Collected Poems

A list of books in the series appears at the end of this book.

Collected Poems

Don Gordon

Edited and with an Essay by Fred Whitehead

University of Illinois Press • Urbana and Chicago

Manufactured in the United States of America
C 5 4 3 2 1

♾ This book is printed on acid-free paper.

Frontispiece courtesy of the photographer, Richard Nickson.

Library of Congress Cataloging-in-Publication Data
Gordon, Don.
[Poems]
Collected poems / Don Gordon ; edited and with an essay by
Fred Whitehead.
p. cm. — (The American poetry recovery series)
Includes bibliographical references and index.
ISBN 0-252-02859-7 (cloth : alk. paper)
I. Whitehead, Fred. II. Title. III. Series.
PS3513.05775A17 2004
811'.54—dc 1 2003001345

CONTENTS

Civilian Poems (1946)

Displaced Persons (1958)

On the Ward (1977)

Excavations (1979)

The Sea of Tranquility (1989)

EDITOR'S PREFACE

In 1984, after learning about Don Gordon from the poet Thomas McGrath and reviewing his poetry in my literary magazine *Quindaro,* I wrote a long essay on his work to date. It felt strange to write about a living poet without having met him, so two years later I visited him in Los Angeles.

I knew Don had dedicated all his books to his wife, Henrie, and had written many moving poems specifically to her, so I expected to and did meet a most remarkable couple. As Tom had advised me in advance, I found them to be deeply civilized, yet Don proved to be somewhat reticent about "interpretations" of his poetry. He disliked what he called the "forensic" aspects of literature—that is, literary criticism, explication, and so forth. Yet he had written me that he did like my essay on his work.

After we got to know each other in those few days, I suggested that, if possible, I would somehow see to it that his works of poetry, most of them out of print, would be gathered up in a single volume. When I brightly suggested that my essay might serve as an introduction to the book, Don's face fell. He asked if it would be possible to let the poetry speak for itself. This put me in a quandary, since I knew if the book were to be issued by an academic press, some sort of biographical and critical apparatus would be expected. I wanted to honor Don's request, but how could I meet the natural need of the reader for some kind of information about the poet and the background of his work? As plans developed for the publication of Don's collected poems, the solution came to me: put the poems first and add a revised version of my essay, now titled "On the Life and Work of Don Gordon," as well as notes to the poems and a brief bibliography, at the back of the book.

Despite Don's reticence about being formally interviewed, he and Henrie did tell me much about their lives, including the repressions of the McCarthy period of the 1950s. Eventually, at Henrie's urging ("for the sake of the children," she insisted), Don consented to an interview through the oral history program at the University of California at Los Angeles, which provided more information. Tina Gainsboro, Don and Henrie's daughter, supplied photographs, identified individuals referred to in the poems, and clarified many biographical details, in addition to providing the historical context of life in California fifty and sixty years ago. Tina's moral and material assistance over many years was essential throughout this project.

Tom and Alice McGrath provided insights into Don's life and work. Sara Cooper and others on the staff of the University of Southern California Library for Social Studies and Research revealed the rich textures of radical cultural life in Los Angeles and supplied copies of scarce journals from the library's holdings, matched by its exhibits and continuous record of activism in the community.

The poet and writer Richard Nickson gave me a list of apparent typographical errors (a short list, I must add) in Don's books. John Crawford, the legendary publisher of West End Press, kindly searched out and gave me a photograph of Don and Henrie with Tom and Alice McGrath, taken on the deck of the Gordon house at 6853 Pacific View Drive.

Ted Watts, a researcher and expert on labor history, shared his indexes of *New Masses*. Pat and David Brodsky assisted with translations of titles of Don's poems that were published in Russian in a volume edited by Georgi Zlobin and Oxana Kirichenko. Doug Wixson put me in touch with Sanora Babb, another Los Angeles writer and a friend of Don. Robert Edwards's *Pemmican* (first an annual printed anthology of poetry, now on the Internet) has steadfastly preserved and extended the radical tradition of the small press literature, including the work of Tom McGrath and Don Gordon.

Cary Nelson of the University of Illinois at Urbana-Champaign not only accepted this volume for The American Poetry Recovery Series but carefully nurtured it through the process of review and revision. At a time when much American poetry has become irrelevant, obscure, or both, this series projects a small but penetrating beacon into the prevailing darkness, reminiscent of a line in "Hymn and Return," from *Canto General* (1950), addressed by Pablo Neruda to his native Chile: "Over your far expanse has fallen all this difficult light."

Statement (1943)

Part 1

. . . other times have sung the rose,
we celebrate the thorn.
—Don Gordon

SEA

Sea is wild marble waiting a stonecutter's hand, chaos crying for symmetry,
For recurrent shapes: the sea is less than mountains and birds
Whose heights and migrations follow laws, return precisely on wings.

Ships etch wild marble, hard prows cutting clear:
Thin veins are open, now deeper than foam; the pattern
Seems forever made. Then in salt curves . . . the blue annulment.

All other tracings pass, all faint designs depart
Wind edge, the sun's point; moon fingers on the tide.
Life is averse to these still early waters: the sea
And the world of man are the last voids . . . pendulous, unborn.

THE WAILING WALL

Harvests pass and turbans pass and scimitars go by.
Jerusalem is cunning . . . it basks at the wailing wall,
It smiles above white buildings, it knows how cities died.

This stone, this native breast, is saved for the hands
Of men untried in action: still the generations
Thump their grief, sun and stone absorb
The punctual cry, the women lean upon the dusk.

Desolation under roofs is agony that leads to action;
Sorrow closed in houses breaks the doors like flame.
Sharp grasses use the dust of Babylon but Jerusalem has wine:
Cities, remark its cunning, establish tears!

NOCTURNE

In the night and the related city the horses of darkness are moving:
Furiously on the ramparts of the mind they circle,
They vanish, they close, the beasts scream and retreat and draw near.

Nocturnes were tender, there were songs of girls.
Earth turned too often: the brain fails the worn orbit,
The eye discerns void and atom, at dusk the light dies forever.

The night is a mirror of basalt, the city a forest
Of monoliths sharpened by stars. I am pressed
Between the night and the city, a grain in the mirror of stone.

The insect coils in amber, years of water wailing over, the airless river
Bearing down. I have been here a thousand years of water,
The bones glittering in the black amber of the night,
The heart a rattle of purged sinew on the spine.

The dream of amber dies, the skull is clothed, the brain spins the night's web.
To be alone, to know not time, to be deafened to motion and blind to space,
To perceive only the images and deaths wrought within . . . but this is the very
godhead.

I have risen from the ramparts, from basalt and the pointed forest.
I have given form to silence, I have wrung kinship
With godhead, out of loneliness understood gods.

THE GARDENS OF THE SEA

No star descends, nor the closest moon, nor slightly the sun.
The casual great sea flowers open their languid mouths;
The silent silver ones slip by the fern, the crystal fan.

The centuries corrupt the alabaster rock; the tawny sea-base
Crawls in emerald and in mauve. Brief are the slower golden lives:
The fed are the meat when armored shapes glide in on their blind eyes.

These deaths suffice; and in the dark lanes, the accustomed war.
Planets may cool, systems flicker out, new races inhabit the land:
No other plane excites the seascape, the unlit world.

LEGEND OF AMBER

Desolation falls in the Chinese rain, sorrow is the sound of the wind.
Rich are the roots that feed on buried nations; their spirals
Bloom in branches, the leaves descend like pity.

Remembering birth, the departures of men, the child
Fallen in the village, the columns endure at the river's edge:
The solid cry rolls under waters . . . amber is the agony of trees.

The grace of amber, surpassing light, awaits the compassionate,
The pure: the memories of trees shall circle her throat; curled
On the shadow in gold, the signature of time.

Now one are beauty and the curious still beauty of death.
The legions gone have said in amber: no arrogance
Can mar the living, the sorrow of man is borne on her breast.

IMAGE OF GOLD

I said: the heart shall be less. It has been at flood,
Now the escarpment will hold the bound river.
I respect the natural tides: the heart shall be charged with blood.

A dream decays, that is all, there is a death to music.
I am sickened by the waves; after them the childish foam.
Silence is enough, the mind is released from the galleys.

I had earth, the impartial wind, the birth and the expiration of suns.
Only the brain lived: the bees of thought were mighty in the hive;
Honey was on the flashing feet; there was time for the amber taste.

This, I said, is good: the tracing of stars, the awareness of atoms;
Salt of the wind in the nostrils, soundless day and the night;
The heart not sleeping, not waking, as music and the dead.

Not by the flags in drama, nor the hoofs of the youthful horses
The silence was taken: only the indolent month,
Only in April her unbound hair, the image of gold in the rain.

Still are there births and expirations of the sun;
Still the salt and the wind, the honey cool in the hive;
But final is laughter, final the beauty of gold.

NOR ANY WORD IS SAID

The sounds of man are to persuade the darkness: the articulate
Have fearful deities; words are burnt offerings on their cairns.
The great realities are quiet: stealthy the planet, the lucid star, the appearance of light.
Time is unwitnessed; its sandals pass, nor rustle once, nor turn.

The cities, the moving metals, cry in the hundred tongues;
The towers, as of Babel, are stricken with voices, the sky is lost to the builders.
None hears the orbit, the nimble atom, the asteroid in droves;
Nor any wind is loud in space, nor any word is said and all is said.
So the heart speaks with silence, the heart answers: the quieter than light.

ATOMIC THEORY

We run between cloudy poles: birth and death
Receding forever before the eye; we know
The lung's need, only the blind motion.

Sharply in the side of the runner the dread of oblivion
Raddles like fire: the lovers are locked in passion and fear;
The child is a gesture, flung in the path of the night.

(Give me valor and I have no need of gestures:
Valor is running alone between two oblivions.)

I absorb light, I know temperature in its extremes;
I drink at the wellsprings of all seasons;
Through the five senses, the pliable funnels,
I pour the outer world and circle it with my name.

Uniquely upon this circle, the atoms lodged in this brain,
I impress myself as intaglio incised in stone: they may be uneasy
In separate space, cluster like bees at the abandoned hive.

SKYWARD THE MOTE

Skyward the mote, the sea and the stream: they return from the quiet cloud.
Deathward the sun as light appears in tree and wing and tread.
The fruit of the tree is the wing's power, sinew in the name of man.
The heart and the moveless wings are loam, and there is grass.
(Nor is there less nor more.)

The blood seems lasting and deep, yet poured in the later vein
Is equal to life. Fear is not privately born at every birth,
Nor hate, nor love; at any death they do not die.
Thought is in transit; and pliable as cloud, the dream.
(Nor is there less nor more.)

The islands are fat on the deaths of polyps unseen;
Yet lacking, had been formless sea. We seem to walk alone
But the years are the footfall: there is an echo not heard,
A wave finer than the eye. We would think unrestrained,
Yet the brain has the imprint of others, it is wrought in their image.

The sun nears the core: yet the last ray is reckoned.
The man is apt in his hour, the grass in its time.
The word issues from sound into meaning, and is remembered.
(Nor is there more nor less.)

KRONOS

The brain marches without drum, it leaves no footprint in the dust
Of buried worlds. All deities are stricken in their age, the star
Is calmly weighed. Space puckers like fruit, and light is another motion
Crawling the mighty rind. Ghost after ghost, the old realities depart.

Now the wise men come to the end of Time: the universe is tossed
In its sleep; all bodies, clouds, moons and motions move; in space
A point passes like a river, earth is in action on the tide,
The constellations roar on their blind errands. Time is relative:
They topple from the pantheon the great Kronos, the last Greek.

Still the dial measures in bronze, still the garden is flower and bee.
Moves over the roots and the Roman hours something in silence:
And the leaf is blown, the autumn bee is crisp, the rust invades the bronze.

We have eaten: hunger is not in us. We have fought:
The weapons repose. We have loved: love is a word, a wind.
Something goes quietly, goes footless in the world.

CONTENT OF THE WIND

Let the friend die and the lover die: death is another birth
For nitrogen and carbon, the elements are content of the wind.
Body alone is shaken by pulse, only the brain
Is stress; simplicity was first and is restored.

Law is a rack for the mind and the bone but elements
Rest on the law as the foam on the sea. The electron purrs
On its orbit, the atom is serene. What had the involute heart?

They remember space, the atoms strain for the lawful star-work,
The massive rings. Sinew turns: they turn with the convolutions. The voice
Is heard; it is not they who cry. Let these go that were not friend
Nor lover, the hand taken, nor the mouth you knew.

Planets make no outcry in their grooves nor the concourse of stars.
Space is bloodless, dreamless; the universe has no laughter, no tears.
Die; let the friend die and the lover die; chemistry
Is not kind nor unkind, atoms have no quick to bare.

YEAR OF GRACE

Incessantly the root and the leaf unwind, the flower expels the pollen
The earth bares an exhausted breast. Man is cunning in the year
His land is fallow: it will breathe light, in grace drain the long rain.

Sound breaks the quiet house; iron rises in towers; nations are born;
Shouts and weapons rock the plazas. Sky is severed by prows; planets hum
On their voyage; the globe, like a tired horse, turns in its traces.

Speak to men or to God or to gods: as land pleads, as the seeds rattle
And fail, so the brain is stunned, the heart withers.
Give us our year of grace: from the nagging forms of motion . . . from time
In its space . . . from sound and the terror of lights.

We shall see if the hand remember, the ear be delicate,
The vision abandon the eye. We shall know if the brain
Be more than a labyrinth, the heart than a chamber of blood.

Part 2

I saw the core of fire in dust of conflict,
core of light in dust of mobile feet.

STATEMENT

We are the builders by destruction; upon us the later towers.
We are the edged and separate atoms; beyond us the element.
We are the fragments, the star-broken; after us the useful suns.

This, you said, was world: ghosts and credos on their knees;
Life in its marble lines; on his column, God. We saw
Blood on the marble; we heard over the column the bleating of winds.

You had roots, you believed: yours the animal pleasure of weeping.
For us not even nostalgia, nor the beautiful companion, dream.
What is to be wept for; when shall we yearn, who are busy with ash?

We relieve the dying with death; it is called relentless.
Mercy is relentless: deliver your malediction to the universe.
This our inheritance: a burden of destruction upon us.
Your cities are at the sea . . . we are the first wave.

GLACIER

Glacier was pitiless in the locked world: the leaf
closed forever, the naked branch expired; valleys
were shorn of rock, the wing was overtaken.

Sealed are the bridgeheads of the nations, the North
lane sealed; circled by steel the granaries, circled

as the North capes. Men form the image of the serpent,
the segments writhe for bread; upon the wind of hunger

ice descends. Northward, and Southward, heedless in
separate caverns, the bear retains his shaggy sleep.

The walls are involute, weapons multiply, the wintry
clans increase; sunlight trembles upon the threshold
    of the heart preoccupied with frost.

North of the mind, the ice plains test their crystal
flanks: slowly, immensely, the seas surrender. South,
the wakeful spirit shudders, antennae sense the blast.

Already wind is blue . . . the bitter shining particles
are borne. Gather all suns and light, the least star
will be warm.

1932

THE VILLAGE

All fangs and thunders slashed the
biped from the sea ascendant,
tender from the house
of waters.
The village was born: for destruction
of the saurian, the mammoth,
chiefly edged.
The strangers of the separate trees
in caverns multiplied: man
was terrible in droves.

Brain would bay horizons: the cavern
ghost withholds. Heart would
amplify: upon the valves
the village weighs
like stone.
Lands are chosen: village by village
the flags declare the biped
huddles in borders.
The nations champ at the bridgeheads:
the sentinels, the iron hounds,
challenge the aurochs.

The biped is lordly upon the waters:
what word by sea in armor,
what cargo coldly
borne?
The figureheads—the metal mouths—
precede the floating village:
the freight is desolation,
the word is *slay.*

They are below the waters: nourished
        in the hard cocoons what larvae
                descend the sea gardens?
Not the saurian, the subsea village
        stalks: but biped above. On
                the mauve flowers the
                        iron is laid.

Nor less the skies receive—master
        of clouds and light, what
                message from the sun?
Not mammoth roars on earth. Yet over
        the cities, village in flight
                measures its contribution:
                                death.

PECS

(Pecs, Hungary. October, 1934. Twelve hundred miners remained underground five days, in a mass suicide strike against a weekly wage of $2.)

In the crypt, for a night and a day, the voices passed,
lamps burning from mouth to mouth. Men could not stand
                nor lie; clearly their backs sustained the globe.

Yesterday a point on a map, now Pecs was graven upon
the continents . . . they taught history to a generation;
                        the document was plain as death.

Night, identical day, the hours ratwise in the groin;
pressure of rock upon air, the lungs rasping, barely
                                a cry in the throat.

The world pondered how men chose to die . . . millions
knew in Tokyo Shanghai Bombay New York London Paris
        Warsaw Berlin Rome: they saw themselves endure.

The moment dropped, and was counted, day and a night,
grain by grain. Belts gnawed . . . the taste of leather
on tongues shrunk to the larynx. Enormous the single
    groan, fallen without whisper at the stone turn.

On the fourth night, the last tenant tunneled the
rocks: no detonation, the minds blasted smokeless
from the skull. The crevice alive: lights . . . white
    bread . . . Magyar ghosts on the plain.

Concession from above: a truce with the ghostridden;
men stumbled, grave to pithead, their women waiting.

Five days: the traffic resumed: yet nothing ever again
the same. Pecs splintered the decade, fires from below
    illumined the dead regions . . . the ruin.

UNEMPLOYED

The man breathes (a reflex, a solemn irony). The tool was trimmed
To one edge and use: tool without task is for the moment dead.
The man is in himself, the seed rattles in the house unbroken.

This was a column revolving on the axis of a task.
The halt was in midturn, the catastrophe struck at noon:
This is a man stunned and moveless at the source.

He absorbs air, flesh, plant, he walks at intervals; but the window
Is closed, nor (for the moment) men exist nor light is flowing.
The heart spins on its own weight, a knot in the iron web.

Life was in the first seas, continued airward, slid the earlier rock.
Afterward: wings, the flying, unwound lengths, the stolid feet.
Later the cities, the men and their sustenance, a planet taken.

This was a point in the line of motion, a man continuous.
The continuity is cut, the point in motion is unbound:
Time howls in the ear of the figure, as space thwarts the polyp alone.
This is man trimmed to one edge and use, this the consummation of the seas.

HUNGER MARCH

The streets are aware
of the absence
of drums;

Not the heralds
precede
nor declare;

Not the stallions
the black manes,
the gold.

The long men stride
between the hapless city
and the sun.

Mammoth is born
of the hardest womb,
walks with a single thud.

(The triangles:
solid: of stone: kneel
on the desert kings.
Ashur
the winged bull
is bas-relief.
The Greeks
die
in their marble.)

These are not slain
in fragments nor worked
in stone.

This is
the last
procession,

The pace
not measured
unwinds the world.

THEY HAVE COME FOR THEIR ANSWERS

The arts curl in the navel, the seven Brahmins burden their haunches in self-
respect.
The people, the drumbeats of hunger, invest the tower inviolate, whence issue:
The preoccupations; the odor of garlands; the hundred years' decay.

Forsake the sea in its frame, the angels, pastorals, recurrences and genuflexions;
The faun is inert in the thicket, prone the centaur between the four hoofs.
Abandon the statue of the statesman, the lovers, the nymph unequal to the
bronze.

Quiet the minuet, silence myth; the great waves and the cymbals perish.
The hour deserves the dance in parallel, the Greek will not awaken.
Nor phrase the private darkness nor tend the flower of death.

The empires of the dying summon the sleepers! Cancel all dreams,
Conquests, balances: they have come for their answers.
Nor evade nor charm in the immemorial delicate fashion;
Nor deny . . . in the presence of hunger . . . beauty is the second wound.

INSTANT OF LIGHT

That day the city turned on the bone axis: motion, and no laughter.
The city was in myself, in rage privately muffled.
No anger of multitudes in the stone heart beat about me.

Later the street, the sun lost and buried in all buildings,
The night stumbling toward fury, perhaps toward sleep.
Then the instant of light, the gold motes
        falling, the blue area open . . .

        in the sky (or behind the
        sultry eyelids) stood the
        peasant, the man tawny in
        some land . . . also weary
        of the day, his night heavy
                upon him;

        speech was in that presence
        over the city; by his smile
        he knew me; we were together.

He answered separateness, briefly affirmed the round world,
Then was gone in space, or behind the iris knelt and faded.
The solitary rage with millions henceforth merged: I saw
The core of fire in dust of conflict, core of light in dust of mobile feet.

SARGASSO

The weedchambers wait, the tireless infinite subsea:
        the corsair must drop in his
        armor, a golden hull succumb.
The knuckles of the sea bind like death: once opens
        the shell of the lower
        water, closes once the
                soundless rim.

Some shall breathe in Sargasso, some shall rise
after the ponderous
the unerring spiral
fall.
Who denied the weed will discover no airward pass;
never the masters,
bland in the gale
and richly weighed.
Nor the lifelong passive arms undo these waters,
nor the sea gazer
untangle the lane.
Men in the nocturnal hold endure not labyrinth
nor tomb: there is no terror
in the unlit wells, they are
home in the airless room;
weedfingers casual, to throats
that knew the iron; live steam
buckled the heart, welcome are
the relieving waters.

Stripped to skeleton, to leanest flesh, they
will cleave the blue mouth upward,
sunder the massive planes, emerge

like shouting seagods, suckled
at maelstrom, sired by Sargasso
father of depths.

UNDERGROUND, 1935

Now imminent on earth the enemy in tunics: hussars have taken the mainlands.
It is the lost season west of the red star but our years
Rumble on caissons—subterrain, the single muscle, the manifold heart.

Berlin applauds at the opera. The war below gives passwords
Through quiet doors—the press turns urgently in oil.
Nights are alive ten paces under Brandenburg Gate: mornings rise
Between bayonets—but the walls speak. They will break the bronze horses.

Herr Strauss relieves the capital: wine is taken in Vienna
Boldly by light, the howitzers drawn in the lair. Yet they remember
The Karl Marx—the detonations still in ghostly Floridsdorf:
They build now, from their black base upward, on sturdier rock.

Hussars on Caesar's road but there are seven hills in Rome,
The guardsmen dream at intervals. They spread fire in the dark,
Knowing the jagged forum dead, seeing no god great in the empire.
They ferment in catacombs—some will bear witness at the graves of giants.

Cleverly again the castanets, Seville nods on its balconies.
Music after burial in Asturias, but they listen in the mines
For messenger from Madrid. Spain basks, muzzle to Africa:
City and land drum their own anthem heavily under night.

The generals lift two-handled swords. The guns too may utter both ways.
No lantern is under Tokyo, no cherry blossom falls upon thinkers
Of dangerous thoughts: but they breathe equally in dark orchards;
Some stars yield light below—tomorrow they stand on the terraces.

Heads stare from the gate posts of the river cities yet they salute.
In the basements of Tientsin, sub-Canton will issue steel.
They die by the hundred cuts, but nocturnal papers pass in the marketplace.
They know death who sleep at the Yellow River: the dragon will disturb his ash.

Now imminent on earth the enemy in tunics: hussars have taken the mainlands.
It is the lost season west of the red star but our years
Rumble on caissons—subterrain, the single muscle, the manifold heart.

EXAMPLE OF THE SUN

The light is delivered in turn over hemispheres to the land and the sea.
The flowers and the life in waters use the sun, the flower and the life on earth
In common: no tree complains, nor grasses hoard beyond the root.

Men bend alike in the one wind, receive the light in portion. Before birth is the
first
Collective: in the brute hollow curled and blind. The second is after the time of
awareness:
Death drops irreversible proof among the bodies of our loves and hates.

The time of awareness, touched by the hand, informed by the eye,
Is indisputable, ours, in the period of mutual breath.
The domain is lighted, warmed, incised in the whole design: this we minister.

Sharply against the swinging light, the armed silhouette against the air:

children in gas masks delicately to school . . . the grammar, the bayonet, the uses
of the sky;
gauze and iodine stored for three days' waiting, the civilian refuge is rehearsed at
noon;
the wheat in the field on private maps, the ore in the earth, the oil lakes under the
gold;
the militia is burnished at fall maneuvers, the riot guns delivered;
the warm atoll, the ice lane, the impassive sea are assessed;
the fleet under full steam the depth charge
lowered the plane carriers theoretically
demolished twenty-four hours before the
declaration.

We minister the time of awareness with our especial stress:
The armed silhouette replies with vomit gas and iron
To air in common, birth and death, the massive example of the sun.

Testament

We slough decades, we the people of words stand unbound in the skull.
We the people of images, being finally of sound mind, forsake ourselves.
In the brief pause of war, hear us creep down the immaculate stairs.

We are breaking the superstructure, the old men fall from our shoulders;
We cleave to the core of our own time, we will yet find the people
Where yesterday and tomorrow open their smoky passes.

Bodiless   dissociate
we have spoken to ourselves a thousand years:
Ego, the pointed worm, consumed in the marrow its own length
A hundredfold, left our bones translucent for every wind to peer.

Eaten within, hollow as skeleton with grubs, how shall we stand among you?
Enough of man was left, perhaps, to recreate himself from memory.
More probably a blood transfusion: the fluid flows in masses.

Justly on the black road each light is dubious:
The burden of proof upon us, we accept with the word and the act.
Measure both in hard scales, some will be wanting;
The others have taken themselves . . . the first redoubt.

LAW OF FLIGHT

The time divides; over the slit earth the last enemies deploy.
The power burns down on the plain: it will be taken,
It will be charged with light, or the wolf regains the cities.

Already the people of passage are on the moth-flight
From the bitter to the easier sun, to the hills
Higher than wing, the island alone in the sea.

They hurry on the earth, their backs to the war-lit houses.
None pursues: the law is its guardian, weighted like the albatross.
They will not die simply, with rifles voiding the dawn.

It is possible on the moth-flight to exclude noise and the rude visions.
The eyes will be fed on the spare mountains, the ears on the droning of the sea.
There will be the breath coming, the breath going: no wars: no stress.
It is possible to live, and to be dead . . . the viscera
Continue the previous man; and briefly the hair grows.

WE SPEAK OF ACTION

Your brain on its spiral still in the socket; measured by space or change
Not an inch forward. There must be an end in action, else adore the bronze:
Mr. Rodin's Thinker sits in the museum portico, immobile, monstrous,
Stripped of all power and raiment, naked in a cerebral heaven.

We speak of action, not glory: few flags, many defeats.
Later, the nations taken by the people, the exiles welcomed.
No conquest: the structure regained, also the bones of comrades.

You fear melodrama: shouts by night; crowds thrust point to point;
At dawn, the body of your friend . . . History, however, does not apologize:
There are only thirty plots, many revisions by time and fortune.
Reject this performance: the same dawn will find you
Cast in yesterday's Denmark, still mouthing over ruined Elsinore.

The enemy is simple with weapons, and his war-cry neolithic.
Plainly he is a true believer in blood: he is here
With his headsman, the ax lightning to your distant thoughts.

THE TRANSIENT

Walk in wariness among the wires, the land is forbidden.
The highway is yours, and the stone fruits thereof: the teeth of wanderers
Break upon stone, or sharpen between stone and the words of war.

Measure all that is owned: the land's core, the burnished field, the western trees
Bending with gold. In this landscape, actual beasts nuzzle the fruit.
The quieter animal (at the moment) saves his strength for the road.

The paths converge upon the streets of hostile cities.
The autumnal faces peer from the windows in a later Rome.
Onward! these are the dead from the bones out, the windy marrow.

Scan earth and sky, standing lost upon the four borders:
Southward the languors, the peoples buried in sunlight;
Northward the waste tundra locked under the polar cap.

Will the eye bear you eastward enough, or westward
To the steppe in birth? Lonely and stern, the giant
Rises under his star; he guards his roads that none may walk unshod.

Coil and uncoil to the last inch over the cities
And the plain; the towers are private and the regions of grass.
Exact is the worm's view: how far to man's stature?

TO THE PICKETS

Power slept like a cry in the throats of the people;
In the lush pastures they seemed to lie down together,
The many and the few. Now the teeth of the great herd
Nibble the dust, the many-throated utter in the hemispheres.

The gold and the iron music summon the coverts of the cities.
Upon disputed streets, between the towers and the simple houses,
The artisan history hews the solitary line: *who is not with us is against us!*

Strike! one by one the holidays of desperation are declared.
The inarticulate speak now in their fashion, they are eloquent before the gates:
Not one shall enter, nor of the faithless one shall leave!

Gas is blown in the streets, first and the last tears are coldly drawn.
They oppose you with steel and the mercenaries, some will be slain.
(What manner of serf the dead, how able skeleton with tools?)
Iron is familiar, taken at the breast, driven year by year.
Can the spine be shaken, whose vertebrae were locked in war?

They will goad you above and below, until the gates are flung and the glass
shivers,
Then cry vandal and enlist new enemies in the rear. Better the flanks visible,
The armies in their camps: *the gates must be thrown before there is tomorrow.*

THE STRIKE-BREAKER

The body will accept the bread of betrayal nor veins distinguish the salt,
Only the heart refuses. Cry the first law, say it before meals; it is briefly
All your gospels. The law may be invoked: a moment is given to any Faust.

Walk in multitudes alone, by the campfires stealthily;
Envy the deaths of sentinels, the privilege of war.
Ask pity and the hand of man; pity you have, the fainter part of scorn.
Withheld the larger grace: compassion is for the noble and the blind.

You are attended: side by side the faithless, each of his time
A stricken envoy. Judas never dies: in every generation he endures
His thoughts a lesser or a longer while . . . then coldly the matrix closes.

THE ZONES

Stop the wandering feet, unbind the dismal brain
This place, and this long season, are entangled;
Yet chaos is divisible, only three zones traverse the enormous web.

Bask in the islands burning, follow the blind maps,
Withdraw the senses, seal the apertures, shrug, or deny:
Yet each by his stress and stature, we trace this time.

First is surrender: manage an especial valor, volunteer the dust.
One gesture, once cut the nourishing cord, and all confusion is undone.

Or gather your bales in houses, comfort with objects;
Kneel to the arts in world beyond world, nuzzle the seven breasts;
Repose on the cold giantess, the state; embrace God,

The sound and odor of eternity, the love and terror, the delight;
Or yearn for the other wombs . . . again the dark child.

Or dedicate the brain and warn the flesh, there is increasing tide:
The honeymakers gasp in the honeycombs of stone,
The people crouch at their cottages. Summon the drowsy blood!

LOVE SONG, 1938

Herr Krupp is slyly intimate within our lives.
The shells spin westward from Osaka, cradled in trains
That jar the delicate print from the wall.

Skoda was an outland name: it smokes in our sleep.
Vickers blackens the schoolbook yew; Schneider-Creusot
Is closer than Jesus, duPont more immanent than God.

Two cannot walk in the old way: they are counted; they are known.
This man will be mobilized when the accident of time
Has rolled upon him. She will be used in a hospital ward.

Narrow the night, Osaka rises on the Tokyo exchange;
Hasten the morning, they double duPont shifts;
Hasten the light, my love, Herr Krupp has numbered the suns!

Who did not care for flowers, cares at the plain end of bloom.
Who once forsook the people, in each face observes
One now unknown at some blown outpost die with him.

Between the wars we share not life but armistice.
The moment crossed with bayonets must hold embrace
And breath, and briefly hate and all our love.

We wait no fixed appointment with the dust:
Mainly from the last dead, we learned the instant's golden core
And to advance before the firing-pin, before the breaking shell.

WE WILL BE MARTIAL

1. The Kinsmen

The gods are absent,
                    nor even the noble dust
                            remarks a pantheon dispersed.

Zeus, Astarte,
the thunderers, Venus,
the lambs broken upon the marble:
Who answers the roll
call of the heavens
from Karnak to the pole?

Only the slayer Mars
shouts vainglory
among the slain;
His trumpets announce
in the minds
of the young men.
The hoofs gilded,
on the oiled shoulders
the garlands and the last suns:
Which of the young bulls
will you dedicate next?

We are the kinsmen,
the bright herd anointed:
Stronger than blood
is death not pronounced,
forever about to be uttered.
Sons of the western sea
edge, the cold eastern rock,
the strangers of the middle desert:
We live between the breaths
of the old men!

2. We Need to Know

We stay upon
the plain earth, nor traffic
in the Roman sign.
We thought the man in armor
died; we saw in his breastplate
the mole's nocturnal work.

They chose the coast
emplacement, inch by inch
appointed guns:
For the empty tide, fourteen;
on the great seas, sixteen;
the turrets sweep the sun.
They climb with iron
droppings; they hold maneuvers
in the fields of summer,
They practice death
with the sons
of the people.

We are not martial. We are
the quiet ones. Clothe us,
tawny as earth, for the kill.
March us away
with flowers
in the rifle mouths.
Tangle the wire,
take us to cover
on the bleak plain.

We will be martial:
grunt with the bayonet:
write love letters in gas masks.
You, hidden in the house
of the people: instruct us
in war! We need to know.

THE DEPARTURE

"When the class struggle nears the decisive hour . . .
a portion of the bourgeoisie goes over to the proletariat."

We have been among you at the last suppers: your hand sustained
By caress no more among us, nor these faces for the sake
Of the beautiful round eye. Something has expired in the talking rooms,
On the overstuffed chairs, in mouths nightly open and shut.

We break from you bodily: for the headline you overlooked, the hunger march
From the office window, the miner's face in the rotogravure;
For the refugees on the roads, for withered Spain, and for your friend
On horseback. The departure is under his leaden shade.

Stripped, alive, unpossessing, we are quiet after the celebrants.
The blood no further bond, nor habit; never again the senses.
The community rolls earthwide from the mind: a new dimension.

Who is with us is of us, we of them and these only:
The man with leaflets on a Berlin roof; thin figure
Down the Roman alley; the Osaka nucleus; from Archangel to the East;
This man, this woman, who will not gently die on the American farm.

First is the passion, the directed full flood in the artery;
The act and the war from this stem. The concept is unshaken in the blast;
The collective is beyond grain in common, beyond the house with two families.

DIALECTIC

We are too close to our wounds; we lick them
And swallow ourselves. Meanwhile the battle stamps out
The last world; in the speckled corpse the grass arrives.

These hungers, and abrasions, nail each to his own moment:
Pain is a private estate, the mind's boundary at the edge;
But all pangs are derivative, we are history.

The blind snake writhes and changes his skin; the insect,
Intent on his crumb, is bruised by a single undulation.
Our span is longer, the convulsion slow; at the sloughing point
A loss of blood; then opposite and equal peace.

We are closed in the mourning circle, we pity ourselves;
We show our sores, as the leper in frightened streets;
We are intent on the withered limb, on beauty slightly ravaged.

These pits and swellings are in the body of time. The healthy epoch
Has open sores: symptoms divulge in men, the structure suppurates.
It is not privilege nor burden we express disease: it is a fact.

IT BEGINS IN THE MAN

It begins in the man: act by act in five lanes the world taken.
Day furrows the brain, night plants to people and the attitudes.
Time, and the inner seasons, mature the soldier without borders.

The man passes in the cities: bones of children enter his eye.
He is a witness to people in fields, to shape of the spine in work.
He sees the walkers upon roads, the feet toward the late star.
The world in extremis rattles like a pod;
Even this the man hears, and in the windy house the cry.

First war is within: against ghosts, mortmain, self.
The man sloughs a dream of applause, he denies his father.
He honors the men without names, he decides to be born.

The man has seen: images are in his thoughtful night.
He rejects the cadaver, walls a dark avenue
First barricade blocks in the brain a yesterday that dies.

Then people are remembered, a shape of bones is recalled;
The cities and the fields will not leave him, nor the children leave the man.
Remembering, the hand curves to the gunstock, the eye glides in the gunsight;
The soldier without borders marches only for the sake of morning.

EXCHANGE OF HEROES

Comrades they gave us gods, then heroes,
and the statues in public places. Their
        holidays remembered giants.

Maces and long swords commanded the plazas;
bronze epaulet the courthouse lawn; wreath
        and robe of state the porticoes.

The mounted myths rode forever in the sun.
We were to measure ourselves by pedestals;
by grace, breathe in the enormous shadows.

We made history in the lands, our hungers
and migrations unbound the seas: lords in
the later words. Generations were humbled
        before them.

They deafened us by proclamation, they
blinded our eyes with great lights. We
obeyed; we crept in valleys. We had no
        stature beside the mountains.

The globe's diameter draws in, the population
by the last trench is sundered. There will be
        salvos. All statues will be melted down.

It is the time of definition; the pantheon is
unroofed. We spew the corsair, and the orator,
        chiefly their metal horsemen.

The land is in dispute, the power hung on the
wire to be taken. We exchange their monuments,
we drum their giants from the camps. It is an
        end of heroes and the beginning.

We appraise stature by awareness—if we have
heroes they will be stern among us . . . in us . . .
We are together by hatred and by love, we are
delivered from them.

Death Masks

IN THE HALL OF STATE

None decreed a mask of brain, of hand or foot, of breast where the heart was
charged.
The foot bore him, the hand beckoned, the brain cried its command,
The heart said yes, no; and these are gone, nor any cast recalls.
They have let the blood ebb, tissue dry, the bones sprawl and the dust go over;
They have kept this that concealed the man, that held the door of change and
holds it now.

The enemy looks upon the mask, lost as the friend, crying here at last his power
webbed, here dread
Reduced to a simple formula that gives no sign to the hand raised for the clasp or
the knuckles in anger.
He turned two faces and one was of friendship, one enmity; even in death he is
pliable.

They have made a mask for women: she who bore him is upon the floors of stone,
Then she who loved him. One is to remember pain, the later dream, the faith
unmolested
By the mask. The other is to find her kisses on these lips, her face
Still in the eyes beneath the lids, here the delight and the hours and the words
spoken.

The people, the comrade, the foe, she who bore him and she who loved him come
singly here.
Do they see clay, or more or less than clay: of this man's thousand faces does any
face remain?
Is all he held and lost and loved, caught here in contour of bone and brow,

The ridges of the lips, the broken mounds? Do they bring the face
They knew, lift up the lids sunken, in the nostrils set the nourishing breath?

MARX

He chipped
the gilt cornice,
in the long dustbin
of the midcentury
whisked the curly myth.
Facades in rococo
split and crumpled,
brocades and candelabra
tumbled the stuffed houses.

He heard the medieval hound
snarling for ghostly bones;
on the rush mat the equal serf.
The new gentlemen
raged at the cold intruder:
he smelled moats in their towns;
He pointed
to peasants
in the dank streets;
He said the spinners
were weaving skeletons, there
would be an end to meekness.

He charted the rude
indices of birth;
in time's bare stone
slit early epitaphs.
The living could see
their distant graves;
the people besieged the heavens.
Death, too,
was dialectic:
he had sired the spectre.

LENIN

He rose in history's
opaque waters like a delta:
The lands of evening
washed from the sinking hills;
He saw the disk
of morning, the later world.

Europe's dying lamp
was lit by the spark in exile;
The moaning colonies
straightened their spines.

Cool as the Baltic,
he appeared at the April feast:
Large over the celebrants
the grim shade upon the wall;
He spilt the premature wine.
He said: Peace: Bread: Land.

The words ran down
the Cossack horses;
they heard in Baku,
Vladivostok, Batum, Kiev;
On the Black Sea
they heard,
on the Dnieper,
on the steppes.

He caught the first rumble
in the throat of time.
He said: act.
The spectre had bone,
cover, of the living
the steady eyes.

HITLER

The endless voice,
the aftermath of war,
screamed over the German cities:
Discords . . . the blind men . . .
the time of fratricide . . .
the people bound in weeping.
In the hired tunic
shouted from the doorway
the guardsman of the house of gold.

The bitter drum
summoned from the Black Forest
the swart, uneasy forms:
In the Brown House . . .
flares . . . fires . . . dead Wotan
seated and blown upon . . .
sated with whips and groans.

(The masks of great men,
placed in love,
are to remember
the abandoned house;
the clay is scaled
to each vast and quiet room.)

The shadow
of this life
is thin across the impatient ground;
This clay, quarried
in the hard pit of time,
tightens with each strangled cry;
This death mask
creeps upon the living like a scar . . .
not to remember . . . to obliterate.

The skull is outlined
against the closing sky;
drops from the rootless tree
the untimely flyblown fruit.

MUSSOLINI

The taurine head
tossed its own youth,
in the sour dust gored the debris.
Remained: the angry horns,
the puffed and sounding nostrils,
only the squat image in the eye.

Quietly the boneless forum
lay on its side; in the arena
birds pecked the ghosts of the slain Gauls.
Six days, for time to reverse
and Caesar re-cast the die, he roared
at the stones; on the seventh he rested
In the empire
held by the sullen sentry-boxes,
the leaning walls of Rome.

The bound ax,
terrible in the brass parades,
is split at the helve
Against the weight
of hunger, the edge slips
on the Tuscan farms;
The blade flashes sun
in the dense squares
to blind the African graves.

He did not hear
the monotone of women
asking news from Spain.

He cannot sleep in flags,
nor talk at night
above Lipari's moan.
He cannot summon friends:
their bodies slid down Tiber
to the sea.
He cannot dream,
for Matteotti comes
between the eyelid and the dream.
Upon the draining head
constricts from throat to brow
the certain, slow, inviolate mask.
He will be remembered
if they unearth
the small face of death.

HIROHITO

They die at Shanghai,
on the Yangtze winding,
on the inland roads;

They die with his name
blooming like a light
on their lips.

The emperor walks in his garden.
A blossom crinkles on the gilded bridge.
He writes of wistaria, of its brief time.

Three days' salt
burns in the eyes
of the fishermen.

The women bend
in the wet fields, the rice grains
are counted at the evening meal.

Men, the western metals,
are molten in the forges
at the seaport cities.

The emperor,
on his beautiful white horse,
reviews the troops;
The hoofbeats fall and fade
in the area
between two worlds.
The emperor has seen the bayonets:
the bronze door is closed;
he is alone in the third world.

The men have made a God:
rising in his lacquered house,
he issues light to the people.
Blasted by the moving sun,
they do not know
God is fed at mealtime;
Bowed over his field guns,
they do not see him clothed
by the imperial tailor;
They have not found God
in spectacles,
a little man with weak eyes.

The life mask of the emperor:
the walk in the garden
the ride between the bayonets
the closing of the bronze door.
The death mask of the emperor:
the end of the walk
the closing of the closed eyes.

THE DIPLOMAT

The figure is apt in corridors
between the sentinels and statues
saved in iron.
Through sleeping capitals
the golden clocks
record his flights;
The chimes, the chosen words,
drop on the falling chancelleries
their thirty silver sounds.

The train unwinds the map;
the actual peasants
blink in the boiling dust.
The traveling eye is inward:
the faces at the window
barely merge with trees.

Or in the nocturnal plane,
between the moon and the people,
hastens the image in the air.
The common roofs conceal
the drowsy lives; on the night's motion
passes the last dream.

The tongue in the halls of state
ripples the valued rivers,
the exchange of ports,
the somber names of ships.
The farmer planted his nation
in the customary spring:
the grain grows in alien land.

Home with his borders,
the pliable image
nods in his marble room:

Squads close the bridgeheads,
the deathly navies
break the sea.
The mask
is a silhouette
in the halls of state;
The marble room
is finally folding,
the borders cry against him.
He was variant
in the capitals: the golden clocks
prepare the authentic face.

THE HEADSMAN IN EVENING CLOTHES

Their fitful history
uncoils, they count skulls
in the headhunter's night;
They give to murder
their own guise,
their ceremonial dress;
Baroque, blind by choice,
exactly the man upon the scaffold
states his epoch.

They fling
the bodies of the brave
against time's sightless guards.
The multitude is not darkened
by a single eclipse, the shadow
of the fearful men is short;
The iron people
bear in their eyes
all later suns.

Blood is on the moment
the idea meets the ax:

They use death
and even death is in their image.
The mask is established
in the globe's round cry:
This terror is the faulty heart
of those who need it.

THE INFORMER

No ship mars
the world's even edge; this life
is an island in the barest sea,
Cut by the fatal current
from all mainlands, all deltas
rich in their people.
He stares at his knees,
a minor uncarved stone
abandoned to the gulls.

The enemy used him:
the shell was forgotten
in the next salvo.
The reserves took
the lost outpost; his comrades died.
Remember him the sleepless new patrols!
This cold circle is
an absolute: no window opens
upon another time.

The mercenaries,
the saddest troops in battle,
are maimed in the peace and broken.
The old women shiver
as they pass, their rifles flowerless
at the hands of the young girls,
The children stricken
by the alien faces; they are shunned
in the streets of defiant cities.

Merciful the mask
as suture to the wound
that cannot bleed nor close.
The wintry island watch
is done: there is death his comrade,
the birds waiting and their cry.

THE POET IN THE STONE HOUSE

The man is tall in his room,
his space chosen in the world
between the ceiling and the floor.
The solitary pharaoh
cries doom
from his pyramid.
The people are expected
to prove his words
with their lost lives.

This is a man
by the sea's witless beauty
wholly bound,
His speech locked
in the early worship, his eye
burned in the dead light of stars.
The worn shell
repeats the tides: but briefly
at the ear of the people.

The war is a bee
in a distant hive; yet peace
yearned for is beyond this room.
He longs for the warmth
of waters; but no certain mother
is among the moving weeds.
He turns to the last solid,
the immobile rock: the child
adores its permanent night.

Familiar to him
the weight upon the eyes,
and welcome:
This is the mask
assumed at birth, the child's wish,
the whole man's desire.
In these few decades
the helpless singers passed
from ivory to stone.

THE UNKNOWN WORKER

The soldier is quiet in the monument,
his bones spoken over
for his work with weapons.
His comrade is restless,
his worms unlit
by the state's ordered flame.

He is unburied:
scarcely warmed at his furnace,
or coldly prone under slag;
He is unturned in his furrow;
or the tall building
has grown through his spine;
Or somewhere with copper
lately wound; or the gold miles
upon his eyes.

He is unburied:
who worked with tools
in their houses;
Who bore them
in safe hulls
through the night wind.
But he is the man in the monument:
cited for his work with guns
and too quiet for laughter.

He was also the land and its use:
the mask is of structures,
of his huge cities.

THE EXILE

They knocked in the cold hour;
the order was flung like an animal
across the mouth.
He stood with the squad
at the station, in the gray sun
the faces bleak as cartridges.
He sat under the train's
lonely whistle. The great native city
receded without him into the full light.

He met the armed men,
weary at the bridgeheads
of the continent.
He found the homeless men,
the road upon the mountain, the rivers
between the nations where they lived.
Peasants gave him wine
in flagons. He saw submission
gravely ended in their eyes.
The boatmen carried him
in varied craft between the cities.
He heard an era passing in their words.
Age was upon his back,
he could not stay: but he knew
the world of simple men was waiting.

He could endure
no other bayonets;
he stopped on the windy plain.
He had died at the first border:
his bones and memories had spun on.
These fell like feathers upon the earth.

The face unknown,
itself still lost in death,
This is the mask of the victim,
to be raised in the later halls;
Marking the final weariness
of soldiers and of peasants
And the word of boatmen
kept on the lasting rivers.

Decade 5

SPAIN

Then we could not praise them: they were prone
On the burning hills with their guns, and thermite
Drenched their houses. The battle was the pulse of beaten lands.

The year has flattened the unmarked graves, the bones
Are white under the invisible flowers in the thoughts
Of distant strangers, nourished by workers in their bleak gardens.

They did not die for flowers, nor memories to be pressed
In the archives of another war. They wanted to end indignity,
They fought for life and its continuance. We are that life.

We do not praise the valor of these fathers. We respect
That time and place: there was light in men, their women were beautiful.
Respect is not enough: we are the sons they could not have,
The daughters they did not see. We inherit graves and guns.

THE ENEMY

The enemy is rich in houses but his spirit lives in the slums of history.
His pride is arsenals, he expresses himself with bayonets in the hands of others.
He conquers by telephone to the outposts, he dines in the spoiled lands.

The enemy is an organizer of war supplies, of military roads by forced labor.
His paid pilots are elegant and deadly over backward peoples.
He has admirals in his family; they amuse diplomats in mined harbors.

The enemy is magnificent in destruction; he cannot mortise one timber
Lastingly on another. He is geared for explosions;
He cannot open and search the earth, nor the night
And its lighted systems, nor the frontier of any man's mind.

He understands the logic of loud campaigns, he thinks in squadrons.
He is precise now only in armies, he has a mathematical plan for chaos.
The enemy has come again into the disorder of drowning men:
He can command these deaths but he cannot stop the mouths
Of the dying, he is finally exposed in the eyes of the witnesses.

We need to bear life; to bury the normal corpse; to notice the sun.
We want tomorrow to be constant, to see plain houses built,
Land planted by season, and metals made useful in the cities.

Bring the stretchers! Open the windows of the psychopathic ward!
Take out the advanced cases! Let air pour in upon paranoia in our time!
What we want is order: we will have it.

Civilian Poems (1946)

THE SEALED TRAIN

The wheels begin with the guns: blast by blast
the sealed train winds around the throats
of cities, the least farm is shaken by the moving bell.

(One April a tangible train was unsealed . . . taller than a hundred divisions, the
 exile among the dark people.)
The wounded, the unwounded, the heroes and the victims
Are hurried by the great engine; the exiles may prove more durable than tanks.

These curves are unbanked, this improbable torsion only the fit will survive;
The green lamps are blown, in apparent darkness we are dispatched to the
 unvisited lands.
Yet the headlight will rise like a planet, the fatal seal will be broken,
The train will arrive exactly as the station clock strikes time.

COMMUNIQUÉ

The guns are the instruments for the first phase.
Some have the honor of keeping the record, the dispatch to the future
More legible than bones and the howitzers tilted like snouts.
Tell them we lived, in what estate the bravest and the innocent died.

How we were stunned by the advancing noise, shaken by the loss of the
 landmarks:
The public building walked in separate stones the night of the raid,
There was a gap in the block where the man had lived with his family,
The decontamination squad worked in the street where we were born.

How we bore the guns and their deep baying:
We breathed in the shelters and thought of our men without them in the desert:
We saw the women at the station as the troop train slid away and the hospital
 train came in.

We prepared for gas attack, they taught us the deceptive world:
Tell them of the fragrance of apple blossoms: of blue smoke, the maker of tears:
Of phosgene: the breath of newmown hay: nine times more toxic than chlorine:
Of Lewisite: the odor of geraniums: destroys tissue: fond of lungs and eyes.

How the enemy had ruined the fields:
We suspected the flowers and the flowering trees:
It was the doubtful petals that broke our backs:
How we straightened, how we grew new spines.

It was too enormous for hate: but the blossoms gave us lasting anger.
Tell them we endured tragedy and farce: how the actors
        in both were killed: how we spoke grave lines for
        our friends and buried our enemies and gave light
        flowers honestly to the fields.
Tell them to run off the sound track in their public squares
        and to listen to us if we are dead.

BOMBER'S MOON

When there is fog the harvest will be cut by old men with sickles;
The lovers are scattered stiffly as birds in the cold season;
Only pilots use the remains of the round light.

If our planes are waiting, it will be a good moon:
The black cities will lie on their backs under the bombardier's eye.
A later night the bright snarling motors will cross the stars,
The moon lean terribly toward us, the whole evil sky explode in our faces.

Load the racks! Warm up the planes! Wave to the young men!
Know they will die.
Know they will restore the late gold light to the harvest and the lovers,
Know they offer it to the moonless child in the shelter.

THE ISLANDS

They were innocent years:
the suns of the islands
rose and set in our golden minds;
We hid there from ourselves,
tumbling the tense buildings
like blocks to open the other sky;
Between the night and the furnished room
we saw the blue lagoon like an eye
in the ceiling.

The cold cities
whimpered for men
and their warmth.
We merely endured
our people: reality was lost
on the white shore,
Drowned
among the girls
imagined in those waters.

◇ ◇ ◇

The ferns are burning
in the bomb craters; the palms
once profiles in our sleep
Are torn like fingers;
the lagoon is scarred with ships,
the iron ones drone in that sky.
The young men have bled
on the colored shells; in the jungle
with the wild pigs are the black-haired girls.

The enemy instructs in the meaning
of the minor key, the heartbreak
in the songs of separate peoples.
The drowsy golden mind
dies like a child
with the death of islands.

THE BLACK PILOT

The plane is a starlike motion; he is quiet and exact in its heart.
The serf is released for the wars: the flags they denied him are broken out
For his departure. He takes in one flight the freedom of anonymous birds.

Deftly upon its errand he sets the labyrinth of gears and guns;
The dials flick their delicate fingers, the private road is blown to the sun;
In the stratosphere they tolerate the ambassador of desperate nations.

The intricate man at the controls, the great wing span, the thousand pressures,
The interior explosions, lead to the instant of action: . . . *impact*!
Dials, guns, bones, sickening at the close of the instant, drip from the sun's face.

War's end for the black pilot; war's beginning for the next of kin.
Welcome them: if not in the name of the living, in the special name of their dead;
Or hear forever his extraordinary cry, the anonymous one risen beyond
forgiveness.

DESERT CAMP

The tents are a statement in geometry, white as pyramids in the moonlight of the
year.
The mountains squat in their black silence, the tumbleweed sleeps on the great
circle of sand;
The metallic herd settles in the tank park; only the sentries like slow pendulums
sever the shadow and the light.
The war is a quiet and terrible nightpiece.

The dawn is quicker than a lizard, the wilderness is broken by wheels and voices.
Deeply the engines rage; from the four borders men converge in the vast business
of death.
Battalions crawl on the desert's lonely skin; girls are waiting in mirage, the cool
known rivers always flowing home.

Idly at noon the young soldier discovers the shell; it was lost by the sea in its flight
to the distant mother.

He is stunned by the sudden appearance of space and time; centuries by
thousands lie in his palm.
He inherits the purpose of the moving sea, the change continuous from water to
land.

LOVE SONG

Still with arms and legs, and eyes unblinded, we walk in the night on the
California hills.
Remember the remarkable peace of those evenings in the year of the great
appeasement:
We heard the unopened war like a gaunt horse thumping drearily westward.

Clearly the planets are unmoved, not a night older the obvious moon;
Yet this quiet moment, held like a captive, is quickly unbound
By the motor in the sky, the voice of the man who vanished over Europe.

The dim city is far from the guns, a hush upon its visible heart;
The divisional convoy crosses the pass like a file of armored bees;
P-38s on late patrol are heading for the murderous Pacific.

There were two companions; now under these stars exists the knowledge
Of the pilot, the infantrymen, the men at sea. We, and the hills,
And love, do not matter to them: they must matter to us.

LAOCOÖN

The first shot was fired to Wagnerian music; drums bore it skyward . . . seaward . . .
Under the water and the blown weed. Violence in the last house on the last street!
The Neanderthal man at the window, the Cro-Magnon at the separate door!

Violence has no meaning: it is noise or motion; it is pure stress.
The duty of the civilian: not to be deafened by detonations;
To plant a forest of silence, to preserve trees of thought for the soldier's return . . .

(*Violence like a python swallows the mind in combat.*
"What do you think of?" asked the foreign correspondent.
"I think of killing Germans," said the girl sniper.)

. . . to welcome the casualties with wisdom, to define the enemy;
To hear grass growing under caissons, to see exiles crossing the bright frontiers;
To light in the mind the violent statue, to unwind the Laocoön.

THE CONQUEROR

The gray marchers came like a fog in the season of death.
The fog and the people do not live together.
No one is here but the gray marchers.

They walk the wet streets, they witness the echo.
They visit monuments, their Baedeker knows everything but life.
They finger the shops: wool, silk, paintings, food, the figures of glass.
No one speaks . . . this conquest is wrapped like a bale.

The war plan was flawless, the general staff received the compliments of the
leader.
But how to swallow a nation? The door they broke down is oddly closed,
The shade drawn on the dusty window, the house grave as a winter's sleep.
No one is home.

The family is in the hills with the fighting men.
The great migration rolled out as the fog came over;
No one was on the roads, the spirit went shoeless to another place.

A land may be taken; but how to possess a people?
How to follow a military compass in the lonely substance of a dream;
How to occupy a cloud, the lightning in the mountains of the sky.

THE GUERRILLA

The trees in this region are tall as friends; barely told from the landscape,
He lies at their brown feet. The quavering earth, the armies on the move,
The solid guns in line, are caught and active in his central points of light.

He observes the enemy, beyond them the forests of the world
Rustling with identical men. His thoughts hidden, the atom is quiet
In the globe's firing-chamber; if he lives he will speak and it will be known.

He is a name and a person to those who read the dangerous map
Of this sector. To the conquered, the people in all kneeling lands,
He has no past, no habits, no face; he is their nameless outpost in time.

His fathers stood against the great slavering animals, the scales, the slanting
        spines.
The spiral returns at a higher point, the saurian pack is closing in:
Once more the knuckles tighten, the centuries are clenched like fists.

THE CITIES

War was on the sea, they said, mainly cannonade in the alien mountains.
The school term is over, the examination passed, the romantic salvo
On the last page of the burned book. War is upon the summer resort,
The neighbor, the porch in the evening of the dry leaves.

History will be simple: the names of battles and the cities
Merge in total smoke. They will be cited for standing in the metal rain,
For women in helmets, for old men with weapons, for children in debris.

Warsaw's fallen masonry was blown up in Madrid.
London is a torn poem of defiance: in her empty squares,
Peasants from Chungking are sowing tomorrow's grain.

North of Manila the foxholes come to light in Moscow and Smolensk.
The Thames welcomes the airmen returning; the Volga
Curves like a mother at Stalingrad, the plain that became a mountain.

The colors on the maps have run together in the metal rain,
The borders are drawn from the veins of fragmentary men;
They cannot tell where Guernica ends and Coventry begins.

DEATH OF THE DICTATOR

The dictator will sprawl on the stairway of the neo-classic palace;
The eyes that reviewed the armored divisions will glaze
On the marble step, the voice expire in the rattle the world waits.

The celebration will be a stillborn feast: nothing will end
But the crudest shot in the dark, the figure with cape.
The death of the dictator is the beginning of war against him.

He was noise on a street corner; by indifference we fed him, by every cruelty
Clothed him for war. The abandoned village was his, the vacant man in the city;
He was the child of colonies, of the treeless border under arms.

The dictator is in us, his filaments explore the stony brain;
He is suckled by the fear of man, the fear of change that locks the will.
His statue is by default in the public park: he lives while we breathe on his violent
mouth.

HOSPITAL ROOM

We need not rudely waken
Nor lie in loneliness
Through the deep and secret night.

Memory is divided with someone at
Birth, later confused by swans and
Fountains in baroque. Who would be
Found sleepless in Italian scenery,
Fondling an iron deer?

Fear is only the brain swelling
Like a frog to emulate the bull
Of darkness. The cat has fear in
The house, the fly on the wall,

Perhaps at its level the flower
Turns pale. These fables cannot
Seriously impair the immense,
Unringing, peopleless night.

Pain is too profoundly shared to
Disengage you from the sleeping
World. The marauder on every roof
Howls the separate, the night-haunted,
Into the common fold: we learn to
Huddle against the drawn lips.

Only those impaled by some special
Terror or compassion need toss on
The horns of the late and lonely
Night. The wound is collective:
It bleeds at the jagged edge.

THE CIVILIAN

The object of gunfire is to destroy the enemy; the vein sings
In the engagement like a charged wire, then the soldier sleeps.
The fighting man is equipped, an element and flawless.

The civilian is a target for his own thoughts, still quiet enough
To be dismayed by terror and waste, the dive bomber slipping down the newsreel,
The houses opened like fruit, the shrapnel whirling in the eye.

The mind of the civilian is sharpened even by distant battle:
It worms through the deadly music, the fashionable round words,
The flags draped on reality as a corpse is lowered at sea.

The civilian is useful who accepts the creative guns; who sees in destruction
The building not yet risen on the ruins; who walks humbly over the rib-cages
Of the heroes to the white city; who knows he may have to take it by assault.

THE SECOND BATTLE OF WARSAW

In the fifth winter some were troubled by the spring of the year that was passing;
Some remembered the foreign city, the black quarter where men were unburied;
Some imagined the remaining trees were seeking to bloom when the rubble
blew up.

It is not the spare facts that haunt us: they are nearly lost in the wild labyrinth
Of the year. It is not even a story. It is an act, an outline of a grave:

April 19   thirty-five thousand Jews
opened fire on the Germans from the
tenements of the Warsaw ghetto

the destructive power of the Third
Reich closed on the circle of stone
the water mains were cut   the Jews
fought to the end

May 25   silence was shed as from
a lamp in the smoking street   the
wounds of Europe were open

Surrounded in the wrecked city, invoiced as freight from the occupied lands,
A secret weapon was assembled among them. Afterward it was not found
In the ruin; nor was a casual flame lit at the tomb of the unknown civilian.

The second battle of Warsaw cannot terminate as a work of art;
It would be presumption to build a monument over that extreme spirit.
The brain alone will not find the point of their insistent death;
The heart must come from exile to give us peace.

The dead of Warsaw, with us or without us, enter the legends of the people,
The sleepless colonies, the men resistant on all racial islands,
The solid continents emergent from the age of broken stone.

THE UNDEFENDED

The bird and the snake are established in the attitude of approaching death:
One with wings unhinged, the pulse ticking wildly, the eyes compelled by the
black tongue
While the cold one, in full authority coiled on himself, examines the undefended
breast.

Drop the raised light of pity, break the classic figure into actual parts:
The victim only dies. The tiny bones lead to the insanity of the jungle:
The victor, drowsy and corrupt, is tossed on the superior horns.

The rope, coiled in the world's shadow, compels the eyes of minor races;
The cold nations unhinge the wings of the colonies before they spring;
The heart of the people constricts, the unreturnable blood is drained from those
lands.

The snake swallows the song he does not understand; men can hear the faintest
music.
The passion to destroy the undefended will not be quieted by open veins:
Shatter the classic figure or go mad in the jungle, the skin will blow under the
rocks.

THE HOUSE

When they fired guns in those countries the door
of the peaceful house admitted us daily like a
dubious eye; we irritated the wooden lid.

Perhaps the house was the mote in our own disordered
eyes; we or the structure were blown through the
looking glass and came out on the changed side.

The air in cubic feet remained constant, still
the eastern windows involved the sun; the building
was simply for love to live in, a tall tree cut
squarely against the weather.

There was a third tenant, an enigma before men were
armed in a season of weapons: was the house to keep
something in or to keep something out?

The weather could be excluded, not the mountains
where the assault squads were fed by parachute;

Seen through the cracks in the dry rooms, the river
crossings were black with automatic riflemen;

The peasants spoke in their languages at the threshold,
and the people of the burned capitals.

The house toppled on the crowded shore.

It was the end of the age of the separate crustacean:

We went inland with the vertebrates, the unarmored,
from the shellbound sea.

THE BEACHHEAD

Study for the duration the amphibious attack in the late hour of the night;
Listen in your beds for the sea artillery; note at breakfast
The neolithic foxholes advance like footprints on the deadly bush.

Afterward the soldiers will merge indivisibly with us; it will be quieter
In the world but the gritty shores of the mind will remain to be taken;
On that interior beach we meet the final enemy whose face is like our own.

The sand is thick as the past in the wasted brain;
The brilliant coral, sharp in the old waters, can impale
Even combined operations upon the mauve beauty of polyps in decay.

This coast has been seen before, some have stood on the edge of the crumbling
land;
The jungle is uncut by the bravest. The dead hand of the vines

Can strangle an era; the trees crack like thought in the dry earth,
The habit of obedience coils dreamily under the leaves of the wild poppy.

Prepare other weapons for the attack on the last beachhead! Grind the word to a
point,
Set the will like a gunbarrel in a handy stock; comradeship is a favoring wind
On the flags of the landing party, the armies of occupation can only advance
together.

THE GERMAN

Fearless on a day of wind
the child of the free peasant
sings in the winter forest.

Suddenly bare of snow
the German soldier leans
on the tree as though alive:

the museum of natural history
saved the insignia, the boots
on their eastward stride, the
tunic as winding-sheet.

(He came in the white year.
He talked under the dangerous trees.
He took the next to the last step.

The Russians passed him
in the western direction.)

Of the complex metals
Of the tables of organization
Of the dream-like maps
the unmelted gunman remains
in the year of the child.

The grandfather will tell him what
is in the forest . . .

> of the glacier: of the pits
> in the terrain of the heart:
>
> of the fathers who endured the
> ice age: of their colder will:
>
> of the numbness upon the enemy,
> the flight to the polar cap.
>
> He saw in the forest the edge
> of the tide, a mauled particle
> thrown up by that weather.

BIOGRAPHY

The mother and the father in procession
led the child to the first sea:

fear stumbled through the new Sunday
world; teeth followed him, and voices
with a vile purpose;

the dangerous scenery fell in his eyes
with the foam, the sea was after him.

◇ ◇ ◇

The young man walked in doubt
on the mainland's tawny crust,

or on the island shore between
the coral and the leaves of the sea-grape;

he made love in the sad light
of the beach towns, in the shelter
of sea-blasted cliffs;

he met himself on the gray coast;
he had nothing to say among the
torn paper; miles under his feet
crackled the blue-dark shells.

The beat of a central heart, undiscovered,
was more even than his own.

He heard noise without sense, he saw
motion without direction.

He found in the seascapes, half-drowned
by sympathetic tides, a permanent
and last disorder.

◇ ◇ ◇

The man and the woman moved on the western
edge in a year of war.

The litter on the beach defined their age:
over the glass and the halves of fruit
floated ironically the life preservers;

in the sand, driftwood, or the polished bones
of their friends.

◇ ◇ ◇

The sea had no anger, no uncertainties;
its wild hours were law.

The child brought to it his bundle of
fear, the youth his disorder, the man
imposed his war.

The three figures cast an equal shade:
the tides of destruction ran without
moons, within them.

THE CASUALTIES

Guardians of the archives: add the notable faces
of the men who stay at home in the course of war.

Discarded by the calendar or the shape of the bony
structure or the eye not bright enough to be shot,

Nonetheless there are casualties never fired upon,
concussions that do not cave in the brain for years.

The day a great action is fought by others, weigh
in atomic scales the value a man sets on his life;

Measure on the micrometer his height and security
when the hospital ship is moored to the side
of the metropolis;

Fortunate, it is said, to be safe on the exploding
earth, endangered only by something smokeless
that blows up in the heart.

A sickness falls upon the half-world in time of war,
subnormal temperatures drown the will in their cold lakes.

The useful warmth only resumes its flow in casualties
who state the facts:

We are responsible for the battles we do not fight,
for the ashes of the alien towns we have not seen,
for the eyeless and the graves we do not share.

THE BEADS

Something can doubtless live in the dead place
        behind the wind;
The like hollow in the rear of war is occupied
        by immaculate tissue.

We are in houses at dry and unshelled points,
        fixed like hens by a chalk line from our
        noses to the front.

A time has one reality: ours is war.
Theorem: three levels of existence make
        one epoch . . .

        to know reality and to order it
        to be blind to it
        to see it in a mirror, crammed
        in the area where the wind was.

There is no exit until the mortars are tipped over
        and the wind blows in the direction of home.
Meanwhile talk is a flight of birds arrested
        by the smell of cordite
And thought is the hero of a serial, waiting
        on the cliff for the guns to save him.

We can put in its actual frame of reference the way
        we lived under the black weather of war:

        in light reflected from the sides of darkened ships
        in ease delivered on the backs of the great fallen planes
        in a state of grace, telling the sharp beads of guilt.

OCCUPIED COUNTRY

Quietly the men maimed and the men dead
are entering the unbroken American houses;
the last march is across the threshold of

these rooms into the abode of the civilian
mind. The tears given briefly upon their
return will not restore them: henceforth

they dwell with us, we are a somber country
occupied by heroes. Arms, legs, eyes and
the contours are obliterated; in unvisited

wards, torsos will exist for years. Who is brave
enough to bring them flowers or words? They lie
in battalions, honored along the plainly receding

shore; we assume the fallen weight and pleasure
of their lives. The hearing they abandoned is
acutely ours, the least sound may be perceived

as music; the eyes they closed we open on a
wider world than helicopters or the plastic
cars. Take for them in the nostrils the odor

of the rain, walk firmly for them among the most
desolate people: love is not to be separate from
them, love is our total statement in their name.

THE ANTENNAE

Midway in war ascending like a rocket, something
is dying and descending, something is being born.
The antennae of the nervous system now respond in
their thinnest fronds.

Later they will inform the brain, the last organ
to believe in change. Radar cannot detect it nor
alone the gross eye . . . like the final instant of
night, already alive with light.

The five senses blaze under stress: the dream
is of epochs. The fronds tingle with hope, the
remote, undimensional, infinitely patient bell.

◇ ◇ ◇

The sabre teeth locked the mouth of the tiger; the
horns broke the neck of the dangerous elk; the vast
stomachs were in the tar pits, and the small heads.

The great animals went slowly as the rock strata.
Men were afraid to move their piled stones. Stiff
the nerves tingled in the thinnest fronds . . .

It was the final instant of night, already alive
        with light.
The flying serpent was broken on the cliff, the air
        contained feathers and songs.
Men built their houses in the open, on the beautiful
        edges of the lakes.

THE ROMANTIC

A village was shining in my thoughts like a ship in a bottle,
The roofs steep as the visible mountains, the doorstep
A lake without a feudal swan. Remember the color of grain
In the valley under the starched clouds, the color
Of the young girls' hair under the regional headdress!

(. . . perhaps a postcard the child saw
or words in a book of princes;
something the grandfather said
or a memory brought on a ship
in a year of migration . . .)

Eroded with the dust of western cities, some unendurable day
The ox-route would lead me into the traditions of another people.

It would be harvest time or marriage time or time of birth
I would hear folk music if it were summer; or in winter
Observe the maypole, without hope of leaves, stand for its belief in spring.

◇ ◇ ◇

Whether the village was in the mind
whether it was in the real mountains
whether an idea stated in continuous houses

was settled by
the Luftwaffe.

It took fifty thousand planes to tear up the postcard world.
We are in actual time and deep in many countries: the romantic
Was only a tourist at heart, he would have been lost in a landscape of infinite
dimensions.

THE WARHEAD

Direction is plain as a compass needle in the English sky;
Perceive the hole in the cloud, the future caught on the Norden crosshairs;
the rocket travels without visa;
the rocket is beyond the weather;
in the stratosphere there is no
morality, there are only facts.

The weapon and the man are opposite in texture and purpose;
The explosives move starward, the heart goes underground;
At this depth we aim the gun at a continent and hit a child.

V-1
V-2
V to the nth power:
death is the international language; at this height
it can be read even by the unborn.

It was thought the brotherhood would come gently out of time
By the public teacher, by good men, by gifts of flowers, and by love.
Peace was dreamed of as a bird: after its erratic flight
It would settle on the white roof and sing to us.

Direction is plain as a compass needle in the English sky:
Kinship will be thrust upon us; necessity like peace is jet-propelled,
The rocket may teach us to adore the infant in the warhead.

THE PRISONERS

The quality of nightmare is incomplete: on the roads
of exploded continents, real bones are moving
the prisoners like a tropism in the homeward direction.

The family is instructed to receive them calmly in suburban houses;
The public cry is raised at the sight of dislocations;
The protruding ribs, displayed for nine days, are buried in the archives.

The blue welts are the map of the region from which they came.
The kommandants touched off the final mines under the human relationship.
Dachau   Belsen   Maidanek   Cabanatuan hide in the wounded lights.

The enemy began as men; they receded to the time of the little horses;
They vanished with the lizards on the bare shore; the last glimpse
Was like the single cell, the uncolored jelly pulsing in the sea.

The image of disintegration clings to the eyelids of the victims;
They know the unsteady mouth of the sea is waiting for everyone;
They know men can be truly lost.

They are henceforth the free ones.
They see us with the doubtful rope around our neck:
what is hiding in our black violence?

We are the prisoners of their broken eyes.

THE THRESHOLD

The mind blacks out at a certain point, only the images of death are lit
In its gallery; the murals we see at night are all of soft surrealist bones;

We study as in sleep the awkward sculpture of the age—the art
Of dismemberment, the separated eyes, the wound acting under sulfa.

Waxworks are shown by intermittent gunfire—
The men drowned, the men burned, the men fallen from heights.
The brain is a chart of hidden emplacements, of people
In the oil-dark sea, and in the heartland the great furnace.

sorrow cannot embrace
the hills of the dead

horror is lost in
the flat cities

pity itself is a casualty

Proud flesh grows over an excess of emotion; the heart,
Flicked long by whips, falters in its horny case. The aftermath of war
Can be indifference, the averted glance begins the retreat from reality.

Nonetheless, as the soldiers have their interminable
bruised homeward route,
Those they saved may edge painfully over the shocked
threshold
Into the lighted rooms where compassion is opened
by a single cry.

Displaced Persons (1958)

DISPLACED PERSONS

Barbed wire is the exposed nerve between the war and the peace;
The mice hear them tapping on it the dry monotone of the cage.
The brain in its double grave emits the obscene word: *tomorrow.*

Wired in the half-world, a house in a known land equals their Father's mansion.
Distant artists paint them, ice-hard underfoot the blue plain,
Or in the bare summer with metal thorns on their foreheads.

The tetrarchs keep lions to prove their valor,
Enact in the black catharsis their lost selves:
        who search everywhere for their mothers;
        who want love and find it in mirrors;
        who are empty and need to be conquerors,
        gendarmes, mercenaries, hunters of pain.

The structure is long in dying; story by story like a building
Under artillery fire it comes down from the tower. The inhabitants
Use symbols as their last food: after the lions, men must be eaten.

UXB

We perform ignoble chores in time of peace: after the guns, before they begin,
someone must shovel the metallic dung of the artillery,
the unexploded bombs, the excrement of modern angels.

UXB in the depths under your house! The state objects to mayhem after war:
the gracious cordon of police surrounds you like a prayer.

The child on the shore sleeps in the shade of the live torpedo:
sweep the holy basins where the successful sleek ships go in, go out;
bring up the mines and the unrecognizable seamen.

Plow the ground in Normandy;
plow the identification disk, the love letter, delicately the warhead;
examine the apple tree in the Spring for the airborne skeleton,
the garland of grenades on the pelvic arch.

◇ ◇ ◇

Centuries of unexploded bombs rust in the pale cortex of the mind:
the dream of conquest rolls deathward on the interior plain;
the tree of fear rises forever with its armed skeleton;
the dictator simply appears, disguised as yourself.

◇ ◇ ◇

All torpid iron giants decapitated,
all houses certified, all lands, shores, and seas:
        forget
        forget

THE KIMONO

Celebrate the season of the death of the city.
Celebrate the woman in the newsreel, the print of her kimono
Burned in her back. Celebrate the bamboo leaves, the folded fans.

Exhibit A, formerly a person, was born as the white plant bloomed;
She is the night dream of the spectator, incised on the lidless eye;
Woman without face or name that is known lives in my house.

Weigh her, measure her, peer for children
in her clouded history; check with Geiger counters
the click of the doomed leaves and fans.

Lost in events the beauty and the grace of women;
Ended the age of natural love as the bomb bay opened
On the burned shoulders: she is now the memorable one.

From the nightmare to the eye
from the eye to the house
from the house to the heart
enter the dimension of love:

woman of Hiroshima
be merciful to the merciless!

THE LADY ON THE CHARTREUSE COUCH

The lady on the chartreuse couch is looking for herself;
Reality is a drawn shade between the dreamer and the analyst.
The child materializes in the sacred twilight reserved for the unhealthy:

the house appears in its decade, the rubber plant in the hall,
the shadow of dust in the attic, someone she hated, someone she loved,
the guilt, the web in the corner, the fear of the hairy insect;
there was a time of security beyond the mind, a sense
of warmth and water; afterward, light, noise, terror, and space.

The womb of the real world was incandescent, nothing retreats from solid to fire;
The earth like a round wind is sustained by continuous motion;
The satellites are only secure together, the sun holds the burning family.
Men and constellations are in hazardous motion, one star is not quietly spared.

NOBODY HEARS YOU

New Orleans spoke in public with the drums,
said about the river and the marketplace;

Memphis picked up the talk and the bass,
said Beale Street, night, and sinful town;

Northbound rhythm to Chicago, big and brown,
said railroad, steel, cattle, mines;

New York coming on the continental lines
said Harlem out loud, the girls, and the sea.

piano said cane-brake, drum said tree,
horn said cotton, cymbal said free

Juke-box opens its purple eyes:
neon face: chromium mouth.

Drop your nickel, get the South:
a kind of music, lightly tossed.

Nobody knows the sound of the lost,
nobody hears them trying to speak.

piano said cell-block, drum said rope,
horn said hunger, cymbal said hope

Nightfolk hear the brass, whitefolk hear
the lighted street, the dancing feet, the psalms.

Beat out the rhythm, beat your palms,
black music, beat, but never choose
those
    nobody
        hears
            you
                blues.

SUNDAY AFTERNOON

Slow   blue   tepid
time floats in the living room
as innocent as soft as smoke.
The afternoon bears a litter of musical moments:
Promptly on the hour come in the dogged comedians:
Brass knuckles fix the face of laughter as the murder opens.

The eye rolls like a marble through the colored forest,
The jungle boy whistles for his lion; the ray gun,
The crackle of the comics, recall the heroes lost in space.

Luckily the hired killers strangle the afternoon:
The man might otherwise look at the woman or the woman at the man;
Someone might notice the mushroom of cigarette smoke, the scientific elf at the
    window.

The man and the woman lock themselves in the room in the afternoon of an era.
Everyone else escapes.
All figures are caught in the act of living; everything is normal in Herculaneum
The instant before the ash.

CRYSTALLIZATION

Expires on the windowpane
one petal
of the hard flower of frost;

This particle of the universe
contains events, temperatures,
shining lines as leaves, as stars.

While a man breathes in,
breathes out,
its history begins and dies.

It is brief: it is enough:
the nature of a crystal
is a quiet cold explosion.

◇ ◇ ◇

The wingless bees are broken
to the metal hive, the state:
they crawl with honey
for the armored queen;
they may not hum or fly.

The closed the dominant mind
expires
in a final cold internal glitter.

The instant of frost
lovely on glass or tree
is apt only in its world.

The state is viable and warm
when young:
in the age of crystal
even the brute stones
are wrung by the glacier.

THE INVESTIGATION

Somewhere in his mind,
Like a lost toy in the attic of his childhood,
There must be an absolute, the secret that will rescue them.

The man and the girl were seen in the doorway:
He must have said something to her and she to him.
If they knew what it meant, they would all be saved.

Someone besides the police must have been at the scene of the crime.
He was on another continent at the time: in uniform, a gun in his hand.
What were his intentions?

When the special and sacred explosive was dropped,
The cabinet explained: it was to save the city.
They have saved it, he said, but the people are dead.

On a morning of sun and birds he whistled in his house.
A whistle can be dangerous: it could lead to singing.
The budget unbalanced   the deficit mounting
          what if they danced in the streets?

Yesterday he talked of the sail he could see after the hull vanished;
Or of the sun like a flower, the earth as circling insect;
Or later in the stone room the men hooded, sandals on their feet,
The book opened at the fatal page; or in the village on a rockbound coast
When a child was sick or the corn failed there were evil eyes.

The bailiff in his gray corner,
the gendarme at the door like a public statue,
cowled or bare, the committee is always in session:
    tell
    tell the secret
    tell us before we go

THE SILENT

The tree is a cone of quiet.
The sounds it seems to make
Arise from the neighbors:
The wind talking in its travels,
The rain chattering on the way down.
The tree itself is silent, its sign
Of life the root in the earth
From which its wisdom comes.

Silent the birdless miles;
Taller than the water mountains
The sea answers the moon with motion,
All its particles self-contained
Until the land disrupts with rock
The huge, untalkative, and perfect tide.

Words are unimagined in the fields of space.
The stars undisturbed by shores or neighbors
Conduct their orbits in silence. Whole systems,
Lit by interior suns, proceed without expression.

◇ ◇ ◇

Now in the empire's lighted arenas
The Romans uncage the man they fear,
Begin the sport of ailing caesars.

The questions bind him like the net.
The questions bleed him like the trident.
The questions stalk him like the lion.

The man is silent,
His sign of life
The root in the people
Of unworldly wisdom,
His tide sustained unbroken
On Rome's jagged rocks,
His interior sun proceeding
As usual on its path.

THE DISSENTER

People will turn the middens we bequeath:
        the hunters
        or the hunted
        express the age.

The facts go with the cities into the rock strata:
        someone is not to be spoken to
        someone is not to occupy the house in the sacred wood
        dangerous thoughts are exported on the outgoing tide
        it is verboten to play with the dissenter's child.

The tributaries feed into the sea of violence.
The iron cells multiply like the amoeba; the nucleus
In each is a man who does not agree with the warden.

They nail in the hands and feet the bill of attainder,
They display in the German silence the broken mirror,
The image of forbidden people.

They need an enemy to tear apart in the mad season.
When the air is burning and the cloud signals unbearable change,
The dissenter is born alive on the edges of the weather.

THE DEPORTEE

I see my friend in a rain of confetti, the comedy
Of the celebrants, bound with serpentine to the fearful shore,
Casting no shadow on their hampers of fruit and wine.

The deep horn, the sea bird, the lighted rooms move into night and water.
The metropolis closes its concrete eyes, the barometer falls, the continent
Is moored to the sightless glacier bearing down from the north.

Dry leaves
expose
the autumn

as little fears
the last season
of an era.

Adios, amigo!

if you pass
the ghost
of the *Santa Maria,*
of the explorer
who sailed too soon,

tell him
in the country
of the blind
the one-eyed man
is always murdered.

THE HUNTED

The one who walks in the river is the constant man.
He hides his footprint from the dogs:
engraved like a leaf in the black stone,
the fossil is to amaze another time.

Shapeless, duly malignant, blind as a fog,
the epoch is a wild thing intent on the kill
before he gives it form: direction: heart.

The second constant is the border police;
they have business in the mountains.
Someone is always cutting the wire, the shadow
of thought is always at the edge of the forest.

He considered the meek, or said the earth was round;
he taught the young men in the cypress grove, or listed
the ape's ascending bone; he entered the dream
and saw the indelicate mother, or imagined continents,
or found laws in the lungs of the English weavers.

someone is always being hunted
someone is always walking in the river

The bleak pursuit does not begin or end.
Guilt, the great hound, scratches the doorsill of the brain;
fearful of air, fearful of light, the demented hunter cannot forgive the hunted:
the man who walks in the river is himself.

IN THE GAUNT HOUR

Everything in the gaunt hour is exposed: the eye penetrates the cellars
Where the civilians defend themselves with charts of incoming planes
Or on the hills outlined in miraculous light the spotters wait
For one hostile pilot to rouse the wild radar over the demi-world.

The children's hour falls like a plague:
The fatal voice cries Drop! Curled as the larva, the reflex
Is conditioned early in life: when doom is rehearsed
On the knees, it is too far to vertebrate status and too late.

The desert surrounds the concrete caves with a ring of pale lizards,
The chosen island lies tenderly on its back. At the gaunt hour they are blown
In modern designs like mushrooms or smoky flowers and dispersed in your house.

As we try to sleep
torpedoes hiss through the planetary tides;

as we try to dream
the rocket goes twice around the globe,
the warhead ticks in the bedroom;

as we try to wake
everything is exposed like a death in the family.

ON THE BORDER

Here in the dusk on the border between the sunlit and the moonlit systems,
Even his speechless shadow gone to earth, the man wonders
How to live from the long burial to the birth of epochs.

The slave waiting the fall of the Roman city, the serf
Landbound under demented knights, the weaver in the diseased town:
How did they manage while the old chieftain was dying?

History is the record of the arrogant.
The man on the border has neither hieroglyph nor forebear:
The dispossessed in their multitude leave no sign on the wild dusk.

He is not alone: the contemporaries appear slowly in the bare landscape;
The roots cut, the hands torn, bewildered, inorganic, and blind,
They grope in the appalling darkness along the path of the human voice.

DECADE 6

When the pass to the sun-drenched valley is blocked by land mines,
When the snipers sit like deities on the commanding hills,
Survival itself becomes the weapon with the longest range.

Surrounded we learn the art of breathing under water:
The sense of direction is hard, intact, and larval,
the enemy a failure as long as we exist.

Whole peoples have waited on the doorsteps of nations.
The Navajo thorn grows deep in the jagged heart of the victor.
Is the city besieged or the army of the plain besieged by the city?

The great bird of the future bristles on the metallic nest:
Feathered in our silence, words and acts tap on the shell,
energy is patient as a grenade.

THE SILENT GENERATION

The old ones are listening like birds
For the sound of the morning sun
Or the young trees growing or the leaves
Or the language of roots sturdily spoken
Along the veins of the national earth.

The young men are growing, quiet
As the morning sun, quieter than trees
Or leaves, quietest at the roots
Extended like fingers for food
Or a buried fund of light.

The stones of the words unused,
The stones of the foreign graves,
Lie on the minds of the old:
They are planning for someone
Who does not seem to be there.

Jet-flown into the future
Before they had a past,
The young men know everything
But words; and the fathers forget
How curt the hour from milk to blood.

A country of silent youth
Is an old man whose sons
Have not come back from war,
An old man dry as an insect
At the end of the napalm summer.

THE NEUROTICS

We gave one third of the time as a hostage to sleep,
Partly to repair the tissue, chiefly a search
For some gold continent we never found.

We met them all in the country we made in bed:
The mothers and fathers of course disguised
As animals, the friends taller than ourselves
In masks, the enemy dropping us from great heights,
The sister or the brother extruded
Like a thorn in the otherwise immaculate garden
Of unreal flowers, of special moths.

Sometimes everyone in the dream was the dreamer.
Still we could not acknowledge or assemble him;
Still looking beyond logic for the sacred ego,
We ran headlong into the night's remarkable glass.

It was too hard to be strictly alive:
From the night dream to the daydream we rode
On a rocking horse in the attic
Of an odd street we could not name.

While we gave one third of the years
        to a kind of sleep,
Sailing intently for the blue coast
        that does not exist,
The burly ones, under our white eyelids,
        absconded with a world.

THE LIZARD

Training the ivy on a western hill in the depth of the dry blue summer,
Thinking of the English poets, of the leaves they sang,
Of all their normal birds, of the dun cattle swallowing flowers
In the innocence of time, I saw the lizard whip out of his flat jungle
Like an enemy, the black sign and motion of the evil in the heart.

He broke into the daydream of the English poets.
He was loose in the world I live in, somewhere in the veins
Or the mind the beast under the dark leaves waits for me.

I went like a patrol into the familiar house, I studied the most loved:
In that long candor had he flickered momentarily, as hatred?
If the black lizard has appeared in the rooms where love is,
The world without it could be delivered to him, he could command the armies.

THE PENSIONER

Methodical as the beetle, appearing always in the same corner
Of the cell, the man in the world-wide stone arrives with the sun:
Perhaps there is comfort in the steady line of trees
Or in the exact view of the lake, mud-colored, broken by the baroque swans.

Strangers rush from his eye in the direction he already knows.
He turns from the children with their myths and painful laughter,
Fearless in the non-existent shell, tender as their white boats.

The ceiling barely sustains the burden of blackened skies;
Night excludes in the furnished room the city of wheels and music;
The man disconnects his mind, pursues himself over the wasted fields of sleep.

GUADALAJARA

I remember the sun falling out of Mexico into western water,
In the onyx light the old man on a rooftop in Guadalajara
Under a rain of bell notes from the pink cathedral putting his plants to sleep.

I saw three civilizations in one instant bound by a simple act,
In a fourth my father in another land at the same hour
Bending over his leaves and everywhere in the dying sun
The old ones of the world attendant upon their secret thorns.

Perhaps the last times must be passed in relation to the earth;
Or the exiles find the only occupation open in the ruined province,
The border of our important lives where they are sent.

It may be a blind connection with the thought of seed,
An instinct to enact in winter the psychodrama of spring;
Or merely to replace in the mind the knowledge of their murderous sons.

EL TORO

The instant he sped from the dark passage I knew who he was:
Defined by the flags, by the high judge, by the smell of people,
He was received like a child in a world I was beginning again
at four o'clock in Mexico.

I charged the first insult, the deliberate cape: all exits closed:
Bearing something evil appeared the blind horse:
My spine was eaten, my shoulder sown with streaming thorns.

Nothing was there but a voice.
Twenty minutes to find him: was it the wall, the high judge,
The bloodshot eyes, the animal inciting with a point of light?

I remembered the fields of grass, the sun, the rain on the birds.
Nothing prepared me for the great plaza
Or to separate the enemy from his cape, or the friend.

Defined by the wet sand, by cigarette butts, by the plumed mules,
He was taken like a child from a world I was beginning again
at four-twenty o'clock in Mexico.

DEATH OF THE ARCHITECT

To R.M.S.

The fruit fallen in the spring
Is a shock to the intricate motors
Of the tree, a loss unresolved
By the sweetness of summer and its suns.
The fruit falls ample as birth
In the natural autumn, an arc expected
Of a circle of rain and light.

Equal to the rock and the wild mustard,
Organic in another order than the laurel,
The house, if listened to, beats
With composure like a heart.

The cave was open to the eyes of birds,
The wall continued in gardens of light.
Counterpoint to the terrible city:
Star presence, the entrance of moons.

He engaged the dark puritan, shattering
The square rooms, the aspects of graves,
Admitting plants and children like pagans
To prove his laughter could defeat, endure.

Blinded by centuries of oppressive space,
The world like a creature of the lower sea
Swam into the beautiful clear lines and levels.
Meant for the great era that never began,
Blameless the structure if dwarfs moved in.

THE DESTROYERS

They blew up the island like a fish in a hole in the killer Pacific:
That was the day the world embraced itself,
That was the day for lovers under the sign of the active cloud.

When the windows are lit by night in the famous buildings,
A cold wave crosses the frontier of a generation in its sleep,
The coyote howls, the vulture comes down from the sky.
It is the hour of fever, the hour to study the nature of love.

Everything is lost to the dead, they are not continuous,
The generals are not continuous nor the diplomats. Fired on
Or flattened or strangled by vines, the cities are restored
By love in the living, the continuity of healing and remorse.

THE BLOW LANDS

Dead objects seem to live in the arms of the southwest wind:
Thorns, feathers, skin of the lizard, dung of the bleached bull,
Dreams of tired men leaving under clouds of their blown ranches.

The heaviest bones remain, and the heaviest thoughts;
The great rocks stay, and history in the mountains;
Stay the hard-eyed buzzard, the absolute sun.

A hundred miles perhaps to Alamogordo,
A bird's flight to the proving ground at White Sands,
A thousand years to the pyramid of Los Alamos
Waiting for the speckled wing to dive, the dry wind to blow.

The simplest act of man is to plant trees,
To bring snow water from the cold passes.
The Indian was a father to the desert,
Even the armed Spaniard thought of gardens.

The complicated mind is seedless:
The simple acts are kept for children in the glass museum.
All pyramids rise in the worship of annihilation:
Dead objects only seem to live in the arms of the southwest wind.

LEGEND

That country fed its priests well:
The meaning of birds was given
And the omen of the rain table.

Everything was foretold but the fact:
They abandoned their cities,
The jaguar coughed in the long street.

The people of the calendar
Gave up to the insects;
The mathematicians were replaced
By the simplicity of trees;
The vine took the land of the Maya,
Who understood stars.

Pyramids could remain, the record
Of believed gods stay in the rock.
A civilization could drop like a meteor,
A nation leave home in a night.

It is not told if a runner warned
Of strangers, of weapons unpredicted
In the droppings of birds,
A plumed serpent like a plant turning
In the sky of the dangerous world.

SOMEONE ALWAYS SAYS

it was a merciful release,
may I go like that when my time comes.
Having said it they are washed of guilt in the oral waters.

The round crackling wreath of sound, placed at the disposal
Of the folded arms, implies the dead is fortunate,
In keeping with my mission I await a special doom;
Meanwhile I deny my own mortality by affirming his.

The roses and the lights are whisked like props in a Chinese play
The gongs confuse the issue, the words conceal the fact: each thinks of himself.
Deliver us from ritual! the great bronze bell of the ego in distress.

It is not release or confinement: it is lawful process.
It is not merciful or cruel: it is an end. The human seasons
May not be imposed upon the actual winter of the world.

THE MIDDLE PASSAGE

I think of the young, of their disbelief in dying:
Someone who is not there is at once a stranger;
It happens to another generation—always, fortunately.
Willing to slide off the ant-ridden globe.

My mother and father went too often to funerals;
Their lives seemed bleak to be so fond of ceremony.
Later I knew they simply went to say goodbye:
When they were old I saw they had no friends.

The landmarks, at the middle passage, began to go:
First the physician, my friend back from war
With the unexploded mine in his breast;
Next the architect, his spine temporal,
Malignant, his houses lighted and enduring;
Then the poet, his sun blackened in Spain,
Who lived among us by reflection for a time;
Now the great artery closed by questions,
The refugee stays as long as we remember.

Loss is unendurable until it becomes a fact.
There is an insight to be sought at noon
At the intersection of the busiest streets
Where only commonplace objects converge.

Here in the inescapable sunlight, discover
You are not the axle on which the world turns.
Abstract yourself like a number from the scene,

The landscape with its motions will not quiver:
The cars will roll on, the people buy and sell,
The officer will stand like a statesman,
The signals will stop and go, stop and go, stop and go.

Intolerable the pain until you surround it:
Neither happy nor unhappy, return,
Relieved of the weight of the axle
And armed for once with a fact.

There are no new words or ways to live with death.
The old ones keep their secret like a cabal.
The ego comes lonely, a recruit to his first battle;
It is not cowardice, it is ignorance about to be shot.

THE EXILES

Every man is enclosed as in a cage
Of vertical and the lateral bones,
Bound speechless in the soundproof tissue,
Wound with a white mile of nerves.

Nonetheless he taps on the wall,
Is answered on the great occasions:
Someone goes free, or the warden dies,
Or an execution in the yard.

He lives in his exile by the clock
Of communiqués from the others:
The flash of intelligence
Breaking the silence of the bars,

The common word of alarm
Crossing the semantic border,
The music of the human voice
Penetrating the ego's even scream.

◈ ◈ ◈

The total exile walks the streets
Of nonexistence: he is the man
Unable to swim downstream;
He wants a church without a spire

Or a spire without a church;
He sees us die of sleep
In all conforming tides
Endorsed by the joyful police.

The cage ironic within a cage
We keep for one who still dissents
In the strangling water hands
As we begin to drown.

◈ ◈ ◈

We may never emerge
From the bone, or hear
Through the tissue clearly,
Or unwind the mile of nerves:

Yet the first shadow of peace
May be cast on the ground,
Or reconciliation, or remorse,
When the last exile has come home.

THE CHILDREN

Omit a single prince from the story, or a scream,
the fox child in the thicket of sleep
howls with the fear of change.

The arrangement of objects they follow,
exactly as the night before,
like blocks that make a world, or disorder.

A formula has the property of magic,
hiding the rude memory of birth,
a bruise, perhaps the neurotic caretakers.

The children at play have desperate need of a victim.
The savage heart of a circle is someone outside
and tearful: the new neighbor, already alien,
unerringly the stranger at school.

They do not mean him much harm,
the game requires him, simply, like a ball.
When another stumbles, a bone breaks,
the ego feels sure-footed.

Violence is the third star in their sky:
they prefer guns, fire, and rope
for the melodic rites of childhood.

The blue-eyed heroine tied to the track,
the gangster riddled with admiration in the alley,
their friends burned at the stake

observe the art of living we bequeath,
dispose like Greeks of the mothers and fathers
they also wish they could love.

IN THE FOREST

The odd child was disturbed at night by thoughts of the forest:
If a tree falls, a thousand miles from the human ear or the ear
Of the fur-bearing animal or the bird in flight—is there a sound in that world?

Six million persons were dissolved in the calm of a sea of leaves.
The youth listened for the report of a single cry from the furnace
Or even a bubble heard in the lung in the chamber of colorless gas.
They went without a word in a country of people.

The man entered the older world of wounds:
No one seemed to hear the wars go by or the peace strangled as a child;
The injured lay in the street for years, the lonely perished in their rooms;
Everyone fell a thousand miles from anyone.

It was late before he understood: they hear what they wish.
He found toward the end the motif lost in the beginning:
There is always a sound as the tree falls, the cry itself is the human condition.

WHEN THE TIME COMES

The lady with the mildewed face
Strikes like an ormolu clock,
Complains of poems like guns
Shot at the dove-colored world.

Meanwhile something like a man is sleeping
Under the beautiful arch of the bridge:
The trees seem to have left the city:
The cold public globes are the only fruit
In the garden of portland cement: if a bird
Is on the wire he is quiet about it.

Someone we do not know
Is a mile deep, and prone,
Looking perhaps for fossils,
Or something to eat,
Or in the black artery, death.

An invoice of young men
Arrives in government crates,
A land mine from War One disperses
A horse in a gold meadow, in all ports
They are still hoisting foreigners
Out of the sea like stunned tuna.

Meanwhile in the desert, by the poisoned rivers,
Someone is counting nuclei to induce dreams
Of crackling cities: the air is bleeding:
In the strategic brain the great illuminated map
Glows in the seven colors of annihilation.

Forgive us
          the daily bread
                    of our concern;

We will, Madam,
          when the time comes
                    consider the lark.

THE STATE

The house when weather-proof for man
Was still exposed to fear:
He envied the mollusc, sea-crazed,
Concealed in its locked shell.

He set the carnivorous plant,
Calm as an angel, in the hall:
It would eat insects gladly,
Devour small animals for nitrogen,
Or strangle thieves, or neighbors.

Tenderly it moved along the wall.
Casual leaves across the windows
Kept him safe from foreign eyes.
All it wanted first was water,
Then from time to time blood-meal.

The house was free of flies and mice.
The roots walked later through the floor.
No one came in, no one came out,
Except the enemies in dreams.

It went slowly into other rooms,
A mouth was hunting in the thicket:
It ate the light, it ate the air,
Grew fond of sons and then of daughters.

Who envied the mollusc in its shell,
Cornered now, reduced, and tongueless,
Prays in the attic for his father's ax.

SOMETIME IN A PARK

The Sargasso Sea, where the lost causes daily rise and drown,
Tosses the weed-wound blackened hills of old minds as they remember and forget
The running of the guns, the sunlit words, the moon-cold plazas of those cities.

It is hard in winter to recall the reasons of the spring;
Harder to bring from the wide sea the face of the water-borne friend;
It comes in the end to counting the debauched and the dead.

They carry the flag through the smoke of taverns where the nightmare parrots
    scream;
Or prowl the fog-crazed waterfront after the ships gone down in the brain;
Or sit on the porches of country hotels in the sad towns of the interior.

Sometime in a park where the newspapers fly in the trees of fall,
The chieftains of a triumphant cause, cowering at the onslaught of the young,
May expose to the last mourner the nature of victory and defeat.

AT THE STATION

Which way do the trains run?
Traveler, lost under the station lamp,
I'm a stranger here myself.

Nothing is familiar except the damp memory of childhood:
The inhabitants are woven in their cocoons; each recalls,
Long since dismantled by the wrecking crew, his house and his beliefs.

The landscape has been subtly shifted, it is out of focus or we are:
Yesterday, manacled to the marshal, I saw the boy I knew at school;
There were trees where we stand, then the sound of hammers,
In the morning you will see the scaffolds with their solid arms.

Who has displaced a nation? The people arrive and depart
On their laughter-ridden tragic errands shot with music.
Nearly midnight in the waiting-room and they sleep like plants.

Which way does the big train go?
Traveler, lost under the station lamp,
I am farther from home than you.

On the Ward (1977)

ON THE WARD, ONE

The quiet time is Saturday night:
the world outside jumps off bridges;
strangles its mates;
or cleans a .22
by emptying it into mother.

We have borders to protect,
voices with exact instruction,
vast electronic systems
wired to the bedsprings.
We have order enough
for a season of chaos.

The mines erupted in dusty fountains,
the toxic leaves abandoned the dying trees,
the B-52 splattered that sky with the young rice,
their children went off like Roman candles.

We are dancing here
in our equal but separate worlds;
we are turning clay into figures
of a select mythology.

They are blowing holes out there
in the jagged universe.
We prescribe for ourselves:
intensive care for the duration.

ON THE WARD, TWO

In the lull in the mortar fire,
        rockets fall asleep,

Soldiers are trading cold rations
        with the enemy,

Diplomats search and destroy
        in the oval room.

The truce is the time to repair
        the tank treads;

In the armistice they bring up
        the flame-throwers;

The treaty itself is on a short fuse.

We have been invited to leave:
        no one stirs.

Once out of the portals they will cry
        "Incoming!"

We would only have to commit ourselves
        again, again.

They have to take care of us:

In all religions the mad are sacred;

We bear the sign from the godhead
        like the entrails of birds.

We are not about to tell them
        the truth:

The only bomb shelter is psychosis.

THE CHILD

Deep as a mole
In the night world I lie,
Buried to the eyeball
In thoughts of violence.

This is the truth
Of the solitary man:
Each is a Berlin wall,
While in the flyblown street
Aggression, loose as a lion,
Mangles the one we love.

A scene from the history
Of fear rises like a star
In the mind of the night world:
The school is ringed by guns;
Through snake sound and spittle,
Through the cottonmouth women
I see the black child go.

Child of love,
Child of an act of faith!
To this light
Even the blind mole may come.

THE MAN ON THE LEDGE

. . . stands in lieu of the country below,
    uncertain, a fragment of the whole.
    To live or to die, to half-live or half-die:
    the decision trembles on the edge of disaster.

. . . is the catalyst of a continent:
    to think of annihilation
    stirs up the house of the living
    from cellar to rooftree,
    breaks the windows by implosion.

. . . seems unaware
    belief in life is frail
    in demonic days;
    one gust of violence
    may blow it among the constellations.

. . . by saying no:
repudiates, denies, dissolves in doubt
all hopes, all fears,
all loves and hates,
all ceremony except farewell.

. . . has power over multitudes
until he acts;
leaps or does not leap,
leaves us to stare at his space
for three days.

DEAD ON ARRIVAL

(In a New York street on an April morning, 1964, a woman was stabbed repeatedly. There were 38 witnesses. None came to her aid.)

She was among the first to go
in the unburied decade
now recalled in the midnight
of another year.

Consider the possible assailant:
hero to cool girls in courtrooms;
resident of mind-blown cabanas;
or great murderous all-american infant.

Stark as a Greek theater
the white of the street lamp,
the noble lines reduced to terminal cries.
The victim was a disaster once;
in the rooms of the watchers
it repeats forever from window to window.

Time was older than Greece
in the depth of the lower city:

the tribe stared at the creature
going down in the tar pit.

For the woman of New York,
dead on arrival
at this X in space—

the decade remains in its nightmare,
walks on its neon ramparts,
waits for burial at the crossroads.

12:01 A.M.

Now anyone can sit on the porch
And watch the empires drown
In waves of carbon monoxide;
Lit by the burning forum,
The last crimes are applauded
By the deaf and the blind.

The Saturday night special
Is wiping out a generation of wives;
Children are thrown like mice from the roof,
The twenty-nine floors of the condominium

Erupt like a magnetic mine;
The walking psychosis in his burnoose
Drops the hemispheric jet in the barranca
With three hundred persons
And bon voyage cards in seven languages.

They are lying awake at night in rows
As on the wards of a thousand hospitals,
Waiting for the nightmare hypodermic
Or the knock of the sociopath
On the sliding glass of the patio door.

Hope is abandoned in the dark lands,
In others a non-word:
They know only guttural sounds
For meat, bread, fibrous or leafy vegetables,
And death in their absence by strangling
In the lethal exhaust of empires.

AFTER THE GOTHIC

The cathedral arises first in the anxiety
    of the believer;

The great vault puts him lower than cherubim
    in their rosy paint;

The buttress permits the spire to enter heaven
    with its fearful plea.

Gothic is an act of faith, the architecture
    of the prostrate heart.

Through centuries of belief, under mountains
    of carved stone,

The multitude lived and died in the brutal huts
    and were buried

In the shade of vast structures lasting forever
    like pyramids

After faith went down with the western sun
    and the fallen empires.

We learned to breathe without the pantheon
    of statues.

We found the continuum in the structure
    of the pulsing heart

When the blind survived in their black places,
the deaf contrived a world

Of silent love, the partisan threw himself
on the wild grenade.

THE FREEWAY

Something I found in the city
When I went to the house
Of my childhood: the freeway
Ran through the living-room.

I remember the lizard I had
That escaped in the cicada night.
I wonder if the bulldozer
Turned up his skeleton
Like a white fern.

The jaguars and the cougars
Have eaten the footsteps
Of my mother and father;
The sixteen wheels of Detroit
Are pounding the years
And the fears
Of the child.

Everybody tears through the rooms
Where the dreams of the future
Are ground in the gears of the iron present
And a kind of children
Have never heard of the past.

It is not the infant
I want to return.
It is only to find a house
Where it was,
To know I was there.

DEFOLIATION

The bones of the defoliated trees
From some deep marrow
Are growing leaves again
In that country.
The water buffalo will not graze
Under the sick branch,
Or the young men move like panthers,
Or ever the lovely psychotic women
Smile upon them.

Nature repairs her wounds
With angry scar tissue.
She does not replace arms or eyes
Or belief in men, or innocence,
Or immanence of deities
From east or west
Or in the star clusters.

She has done penance
For the acts of the felons
By the leafless and the bloodless dying
        of the trees.
Now she tries to live with her grief:
Reduced; ashen; scant; fruitless
        for a generation.

THE GENERAL

The nature of a man is haunting the avenues of sleep.

I see the inscrutable face of the general,

I hear ricochet his farewell address to the troops: *"Good shooting!"*

The generals do not appoint themselves;

I chose him by some act I dare not recall.

Somewhere the lines of our lives intersected, he became

my protector and emissary to distant fields.

If I am responsible for his medal of honor, then also

for his idea of honor and his words.

The nature of a man is haunting the avenues of sleep.

I see the insurmountable face of the killer among the great trees;

I crouch with him on the bamboo platform bound with vines;

Below, in the deadfall, we await the lion and the white ants.

KILLING

If you see the victim
Or even hear the sob,
The holy tides of guilt
Begin to rise and drown.

A kill at carbine range,
As in the jungle clearing,
Needs the sanction of the state—
Can a state commit a crime?

At thirty thousand feet
There are no dimensions:
The Himalayan dust you make
Obscures the marionettes
Sliding in the river.

Progress in killing
Is in the delusion of distance:
The farther you get,
The closer to innocence.

The final solution:
The country soldier
Blowing up a planet
He cannot imagine,
Pure as the great bull
Astride the land of flowers.

HISTORY

When the war begins
It seems to have reasons;
An hour, a day, a week later,
No one can recall them.

The field of violence remains;
The demolition of children;
The life of the back wards.

Strategy arises in the ego of the king,
Tactic in the anxiety of the general.
Someone is always giving orders
Out of his secret depths.

The commander-in-chief, at the mercy
Of his childhood, prolongs the battle
To conquer his father and/or mother.

The officer with the recurrent dream
Takes his ship into the sea of mines
To relieve the guilt-ridden.

The squadron leader, who never made it
Among equals, wipes them out
With the huts of colored strangers.

When the war begins
It seems to have reasons,
When the war goes on
We know the reasons:

All bloody actions derive
From the labyrinthine men
Who cannot get out.

MIGRATIONS

They have an urge to migrate
To that bare and dangerous desert
Where the ghost of Abraham
Blows like sand among the legends
Of the Mediterranean.

The caribou in the arctic crossing
Turn and wheel in their thousands
When an alien creature
Looms on the white horizon.

A mile of birds,
Intent on the south,
Will sense a solitary hawk
And veer toward another moon.

The bison roamed for millennia
Side by side with the Sioux:
The apparition of the pale marauder
Sent them over the escarpment.

They know what the caribou know,
The birds in their season,
The lemmings down from the mountain
In the month of their destruction:
An endangered species
Has to leave home.

BLOWING AWAY

The plains are going away again,
Tormented by drought,
Fractured and thrown
By the wind and the old despair.

The cattle fall in the white noon;
The Osage and the Apache
Choke in the dust
Of their rain-seeking feet.

When the land is blowing,
The people follow its tracks:
The young are going away
For their reasons,
Gasping like animals
In the dust
Of the appalling decade.

They walk on the continents
To the holy land in the fantasy
Where the scimitars of the emir
Mean them no harm.

The emir is a realist:
He will not respect
The age or innocence
Of the children
Of another blasted apocalypse.

FLOWER CHILD AT 30

Why should an old man weep
On a birth date as young
As the month of April?

He has a memory a decade long
Of an afternoon in the park,
Of the sun and the sound
Of a hundred guitars,
Of the thousand and one voices
Of a whole generation
Handing flowers and smooth pebbles
To the people of that planet.

Where are the armies now
Of the non-violent children?
On every street corner is posted
The closed and silent tank,
The sniper slips his thirty caliber
Into the firing chamber
On the rooftops of the world.

There was that great singing afternoon
        without strangers.
He weeps for the child and for himself:
Who will ever again give the old man
A flower with such blue eyes?

KAMIKAZE

The young Japanese are circling still,
They cannot rest or land
Until we understand
The kamikaze chose to fall
Straight down the clouds
On the divine wind of annihilation.

The young monks in saffron robes
Burned in the cruel light,
Toppled like belief in the cinders
On the public square.

The faith in degrees of immolation
Creeps blindly around the globe;
The young of the hemisphere
Dived through clouds of gas,
Fell onto bayonets,
Rehearsed with detonators
In the rumpus rooms of suburban houses.

The emperor denied his pilots by survival,
The Buddha sat like stoneware in the glow.
We fail the young until we find the flaw in the world,
The hole in the fields of glory through which they go.

WE ARE LIVING

We are living twenty-four hours
At a time
In the aura of the unknown soldier
At the telephone
Under the midwest wheat.
The missile in the iron cradle
Sleeps away its infancy;
The hawks of the cadaver
Tighten their blue circle.

The mothers pray for the health
Of the stranger
Over the pulsating heads of their newborn;
Never in history a psyche
So commended to the nurses of heaven.

We are locked in the devices
That protect us from the protectors;
Again in the symbiosis of life: death:
We are locked in the embrace
Of the warrior child.

In the twilight where we survive
The fantasies
He is our next of kin.

If his metabolism is normal
We last another day.
O brother, father, victim, of the era
Of fatal decisions!

THE REICHSTAG FIRES

never end with one burning:
They begin with it.
Fire leads to fire,
Then to holocaust,
The charred bones of a people
With nails in their feet.

The border incident
Never makes a war.
The will to war
Is the only incident:
War follows like a foaming dog.

They are always watching
For an open window,
For a night man sleeping.
The victims, in the sea of smoke,
Walk to the cruciform trees.
It begins in a blaze of hysteria:
Ends in dark and death.

Always one defense:
Whatever is at hand,
Beginning with the stones
Of the long street.

THE TEMPORARY MAN

We think we are here, or there,
Or essential to the landscape;
After all, we have a house,
          a neighbor.

We know where the neighbor will be
When the horn is blown
Over the baying of the swamp dogs.
We are really historians,
In the caravansary for a sleep.

The figures of that long scroll
Are always the same:
In the costumes of countries
Or centuries,
Ice-locked in the brotherhood
Of destruction,
The winter Cossack and his Jew.

Tomorrow the world
Said the German
And the Roman
And the Egyptian
And the Amalekite
And the captains of the triremes
On the outer and the inland seas.

My father crouched in the attic
While the terror swept by
In the Lithuanian night.

I learned from him:
Home is the halfway house to exile,
We are only on leave from Auschwitz.

NONPERSON

If dead
they need only transport his worms
or change the name of a street.

Alive he is a dilemma
undone by declaring him extinct,
as the pterodactyl
sank on leather wings.

If memory persists,
if you consort in the head
with a nonperson,
you can be wrapped in wet sheets
in a hospital room until you recover.

The face you see
in the family album
they tell you is illusion:
it can be made to disappear
with a snap of imperious fingers.

He walks in the avenues of night;
the dog and the passerby
know he has a shadow.

The state that abolished him
exists only in the mind:
when he finds the others
they will announce the nonstate,
the first commune.

TABLEAU VIVANT

The five thousand years
Of the torture light of history
Expose a fact:
The guard is a prisoner,
The man in the cell
Embraces him forever in his iron care.

The tableau was once exact:
The headsman and the head,
The Castor and Pollux
Of the earthbound
Of the dark ages.

They fall in the black tunnel
Or serve hard time
And leave with a new suit; the warden
Is embalmed in the watchtower
Of his own idea.

The key to the manacles
Turns in the rusty heart;
Someone in charge of the noose
Stands beside the hooded
On the high gallows,
Drops his mind through the trap door.

The nature of chains
Requires a minimum
Of four wrists;
The captor is endlessly captured,
Running like mad in his sleep.

SAMIZDAT

They are closing in;
We can hear the snuffle of the dogs
    in the night.
For every knock on the door one dies
    of a burst ventricle.

What do we want you to know?
Only that we exist.
Perhaps you will tell your children
    for their sake.

Meanwhile, words are the litanies
    of the hunted,
Placed on the forbidden altars
In all the caves from Altamira
To the calcified cities of the sun.

They cannot bear to think
    we are alive
And putting unlikely notions
On the kind of papyrus
That will survive the empire:
    again.

. . . is this Byzantium
or did we move to Rome
or was it Madrid
or Munich
and once in Yenan
and twice at Wounded Knee . . .

REFUGEES

Civilization is a river of refugees:
In the memory of the simple life
Of a man
The only river
That never goes dry.

The tides come down
From the falling mountains of war,
From the arroyos of anguish,
From the terror rising underground,
Above ground, in the airbound columns
Of fire and rain.

The face is always the same:
The face of the Miura bull
When the sword cracks the heart,
The knees give way,
The tongue hangs in the sick arena.

The white horse of the centuries
Drags the same caravan
Into the black distance;
They divide the splinters of the god,
The maize or rice or unleavened bread;
On the two-wheeled cart
The mother of the long march
Bends like a mound of wool
Toward the collapsing horizon,
Toward a thousand miles of dying Cherokee,
Toward the river that never rests in the sea.

EXTRADITION

O platoons of secret men,
fan out in the direction
Of the poles and horizons!—
he has to be somewhere,
preferably the province of despair.

Or on the beach in the swarthy light
with the foreign woman
and the wine of the country.
He makes contacts in the gloom:
he is told or he tells them.

Or asleep in a forbidden land
where everyone is a pariah
even his dreams imperil us
with slips in the Freudian code—
nightmares! nightmares!

This is no time to be lost.
Or found on a pleasure boat
in a doubtful river
with the longnailed dancers.

The guilt is in the evidence,
the evidence in the round fact
the secret men are after him.

THE UNDERGROUND RAILROAD

Grandchildren of slaves
can you remember the legend
for the use of the living
in the stone swamps of the cities:

what did your father say
of the night road northward,

what did his father tell him
of those lost stations?

He went down
at the edge
of the cane-brake,

slept with animals

came up in the latitude
of dissenters.

The landmarks of those journeys are needed again.

Who will uncover the grass-grown stations,

What is the address of the descendants
    of the friendly people?

The underground railroad is a dream that never wakens:

    of passage for the pursued
    through the houses of strangers,

    of passage for ideas
    through the open rooms of the mind,

    of one Dred Scott or always another in time
    fallen in the direction of his true north.

MEMORIAL DAY

My God they're still marching
Down Main Street,
Still playing John Philip Sousa
In the key of the year of the child.

They have the annual heart
To put flowers on the skeletons,
To remember the legless, the eyeless,
The reasons for the last six or seven wars,
The uncounted surreptitious landings
On malarial coasts.

They don't know Pompeii is flat,
Herculaneum is finished,
The Maya have left their cities.
They don't know the whole thing
Blew down the Yalu that December.

They don't even see the fine ash
Falling on their houses
And their praying mantis heads.
They just go marching down Main Street
Like, man, two hundred years ago.

WE ARE NOT READY

        for the collective:
It requires a state of grace
Light years from these war cries
On the violent desert.

The people of the mind
Live in its cerebral caves:
When the door opens
On the real world
They hear the nightriding mares.

The shellhole, neurosis, we seek
Between the dream and the fact.
In the debris,
In the smoke signals,
In chaos,
We sleep and imagine the landscape

Of the commune in its glory
Rising with each century
And dying with it.

It demands more than a belief
In our sleep
To enter the peaceable kingdom.
Or like the young Keats
We may pursue ourselves,
A fantasy in glazed ware,
Around and around an urn: and ash.

THEY COULD NOT LIFT THEIR HEADS

Paradise is lost each day,
Newfound in figures of the night,
Once more dispersed
Among the white bones of morning.

The war that underlies them all
Is waged in the serious heart.
We land over and over again
On the beaches of hope and desire,
Only to awaken on that dead sea
Where the fish turn up their bellies
And the horizon goes down
Like the ship of the imagined world.

Whole lives are said to perish
In the exhausting civil war
Between fact and fantasy.
Nations fall into grief and despair
As the armies of the lemmings
Hurry on fur-covered feet
To drown in northern waters.

Dream is the horn of the Irish elk:
They could not lift their heads, and died,
Their young unborn through eternity.

WHAT SHALL I DO?

He was a man engaged in a world,
A spatial object lighted and warmed
By the sun of his own fantasy;
When she had a child she was intact,
An arrangement in squares of anxiety,
And lines of love and stress.

The foxes are still running
In the canyons on the edges
Of the city and the fawn
Steps into the garden at night,
The ruins of Stonehenge and Monte Alban
Measure and transcribe the heavens,
The submicroscopic armies swarm
In the unexplored marshes of the earth,
Islands arise in the coral water
And are sunk by the weapons.

The man and the woman
Have closed the windows.
We hear over the roofs,
Behind the bolted doors
And the minds of the old:
What shall I do today,
Tonight, tomorrow, the day after?

THE FAMILY

Now at the age of the death
Of the mother and father
They often return to me
As characters in a miracle play
Observed in the glass
Of the seventh decade.

◇ ◇ ◇

The child felt he was watched by strangers
Who thwarted his natural impulse
To die early by water, poison, fire, falling from cliffs.

The youth walked in the fields of fantasy
Until they summoned him
To the real world they believed in:
The province of the informer,
The city of the confidence men,
The house of their failures.

When they were old
The man had to visit them
In the orphanage
Where they remembered so well
What never happened.

Now in the clearest decade I see
They were the continuity from dark to dark,
The keepers of the seals of the genes,
The stones in front of the lair
Where the young are hidden from the hawk.
Now deep in the irreversible dusk,
Late, late,
We are a family.

OBITS

Mother's day began with coffee
And a list of the dead;
She had to see who was gone
Or perhaps who was left
In a census of both worlds.

Sometimes she smiled in panic,
Or was lost in a dream of years;
Or impassive, one whose flock
Is blown apart by thunder,
Who will gather them, or most,
In the quiet of the light.

Now I am old enough
To join her grave registration,
To find some comfort, still being around,
Some distress as one by one they go,
Some wonder at the endurance
Of a species that can live,
Watching its generation
Vanish down a hole in Eden.

THE NATURE OF THE CITY

is spare and sparse
And hard to find
And hard to keep alive
In corners and waterless crannies
And gray mouse holes in the cellar.

A mile without a tree
Is not a habitation but an error
In the course of time.
A bird would be electrocuted
Singing to the leafless pole.

How can we tell about the world
We see and hear
As if through window and water
In the aquarium,
Two alien elements between us
And the wonder and the grace
Of orchid fins.

In the nature of the city
We are dismembered:
Now I understand
Our enduring envy of Indians
And their destruction.

THE HOUSE

The house we live in
Is a shelter from the furies;
We walk the floors by day,
We try to sleep in its dark arms.

It is taken over by night:
The roof talks to itself,
The black windows look in,
The knots crackle and cry
As though with arthritis
Or memories of the violent world
It has survived.

When you live together for decades,
Objects and people are related:
They seem to be sentient,
We learn to be still.

Nothing will ever scurry or warn
In the city, no premonitions
In the great successful pyramids
Of the sun and the moon of tomorrow.

They will not even know
When it comes. We will:
The house always trembles
Just before a disaster.

PLANTS

The woman who talks to plants
Sometimes talks to me; clearly,
I have not their wisdom
Or their grace.

Does she address the leaf, or the stem,
The whole creature in its life,
Or the root, does her voice
Go to the root and nourish it
Like a mouth in the moist darkness?

Now we enter separate worlds:
Her belief in the subterrain,
My belief in hers against my will,
Against the hard geometry of fact.

Where logic and dream depart,
The earth-bound, the star-bent,
Rush for light years
To divergent heavens.

She talks to plants and waits,
Content with silence and new leaves
Or sometimes flowers
In the splendor of that kind of speech.

If I could, I, too,
Would put them forth for her
if only for a season.

THE NEIGHBOR

He seemed the sole survivor
Of a dead planet,
Owning nothing but himself.
He passed through the treasure
In the thickets of the city,
Armored in his indifference,
Led by the extreme light of compassion.

No one could endure him.
He said nothing, but they heard:
        amnesty, amnesty.
They were glad when he moved:
They could resume the games.

His life casts no shadow
Upon them now,
Yet something is immortal
In the minds of the neighbors—
An open question like a wound.

They have a compulsion
To talk about him.
They think he had problems
And buried them in public.
They have to decide he was sick
        very sick

THE FIRST LAW

The first law of the dynamics of life
Is to know how to die.
We have to choose, as we open our eyes,
The stones and rituals,
Under what cloths and leaves we'll lie.

The old ones found their ways and means:
Death in the Slavic drama
Stands in the corner, a member of the family,
While the sons and daughters curse;
The small child in Cuernavaca
Chews his candy skeleton and laughs
On el dia de los muertos.

They wear white in Asia
And eat at funerals:
Nature needs no mourning.
Elsewhere, the arthritic
Slip into the cold seas;
Half a world to the south
The burning ghats and the widows
Line that dark and bloodbound river.

The first law
Is to know how to die
Or they will never imagine
What to do with us.

THE MESSAGE

The lines of communication will be down
In a storm of blown nerves
If a cerebrovascular accident occurs.
We will know the genesis of love:
In body, mind, perception,
All of them, or the legendary heart.

I can tell you now
If I cannot hear, or see, or speak,
Or tap in some primal code,
I intend to be aware of you,
To hold you intact inside the sockets
Like the imprint of the fossil fern.

If I leave as a sentient being,
Remember this message in advance
From that immobile world
That does not exist and may not.
If it comes, we who have been in touch,
Will be again, in some singular way.

PASSING AWAY

He passed away she said
Perhaps like smoke
That might drift back some day,
Certainly not like death
That won't.

She passed away he said
As though she came
To the servant's entrance
For an eight-hour shift,
Then ambled on.

The child passed away they said,
Too pure, unearthly—
Not that a bacterium
Looking for warmth, or moisture,
Wandered in.

They will not utter it,
They think it is the word that kills,
Not the denial of the rocky mortal,
Not belief in angels, curly pink,
And father and mother somewhere,
Of course not grounded,
Still telling them what to say
When company comes.

THE CONTRACT

I have given my body to science:
Now over and over again,
The star of the Medical Center,
I lie on veins of marble.

Under a bank of fluorescent suns
The people with knives
Are carrying out their contract,
They are going to look for me.

If they discover me
They will do better than I did.
They will see the landscape of scars,
The benchmarks on the bone,
The convolutions of the brain
Pointing to some obscure trouble.

I keep wanting to tell them
But I never know what it is.
This is the hour when the wisdom
Should be imparted to the young,
The consummation of all the decades
Of breathing in and out,
The eons of grappling for light
Among the tangled ropes of darkness.

actually
i won't even be there

NEOLITHIC

I am turning to stone:
I feel the calcium
Adhere to the spine,
The stalagmites rising
From my feet,

The stalactites growing down
From my brain;
When they meet in my chest
Like the teeth of rodents
I will know it is time.

Meanwhile there is much to be done
And I lurch in circles
Like a wounded bull
Who will never do anything.
I will say something instead,
I will leave a heritage
Of imperishable thought
As soon as I can get it together.

A tangle of days ahead,
Nights when the calcium
Advances on the bone,
Perhaps whole seasons to be spent
In wondering how to behave
In the midst of the new stone age.

NIGHTS

Then at some uncertain age
We barely wait for dawn
To tell our dream to someone
Anxious to tell us theirs.

A third of the time we sleep,
In age the active third.
What happens there beyond belief
We rush to find once more at night
Perhaps because we are the heroes
Emergent after peril but alive
To stare into the morning light.

Or in the dream we manage
To restore our dead
To tell us they survive
To die again when we awaken.

We hurry into sleep,
The land of beasts and children,
The avenue to bloodshot seas,
The wilder part of what is left.

IN MEMORIAM

Memory is a desert water-hole;
It dries up as the aging traveler
Approaches and requires it
To survive in his own person.
He burrows in the temperature of sand
Toward the bones of the pallid lizard
That was himself when agile.

The landscapes are irrecoverable
And the girls of light among the trees
And on mountains and running in the foam
Of the cobalt sea,
And nightmares and dreams of that coast,
And friends and fathers
And all that anger and that love.

When memories do not answer
The summons of the years
We know they are lying somewhere
In that desert, parched and shrinking,
The holy part of our existence,
Secured we thought for the night.

Out of the bloody chrysalis
Into the breathing world;
A moment later begins the stage

Of the second larva;
Forbidding us even our recollections,
Falls the dark gauze.

EXILES

The row of chairs
On the endless porch
Of the house of the old
Is occupied like a country
By shaky filaments
In the shape of men.

They wander as far from the nurse
As they can go
In the imaginary forest.
They are looking in the earth tunnels
For the child they left
On the other side of the stream.

The region they inhabit now
Has an unguarded frontier;
To astound the merciless
They cross it without permission.

The exiles of the province
Of the interior
Are stateless, stateless—
Forever in need of a passport
To visit the land and the living.

70

Seven decades have gone unburied,
Each practice death only a year long,
Another always rising
In the manner of untiring suns.

Or one could think of an iceberg
Borne on that current
To the grace of southern water,
Merely a spare footing left
To keep its balance
While it moves with what dignity
To what end.

Everything else seems to be
Where it was—
The children are small and pale,
The mothers fret like goats
In the pastures of the city,
The fathers are trading cowrie shells.

Seventy is not where I thought
Or where it ought to be,
It is where I am: a white berg
Dissolving in the bony sea.

SNAKES

Now I see the lethal snake
Regards the world with kindness
After he swallows the brown gopher
And lies in the light
Listening to the murmur of digestive juices
Like man's beginning and possible end.

Ideas of a universe
Creep around the edges of the shade,
Fold and perish of enervation.
Nourishment, a mild climate,
Are ample for snakes or old men
Curled in their skins and serapes.

War, hunger, fear of the hawk,
Are last month's crises;
Today is round and full,
With heat and food enough piped in
To be pre-natal, a life
We never really knew
But sought in all our burrows.

YOU ARE BORN AGAIN

When you are old
You are born again
Each morning: in this parturition
You are your own father and mother,
You fear you are your own child.

You encounter the new sun
With alarm in the company of pain,
With the wonder of the re-discovery
Of a submerged continent.

Through the night
You looked for someone
You will not find in the light.
Through the day
You long for the search
That begins with dark and dream.

It is impossible to enter the day:
The population of the night
Is not with you; strangers are swarming;
You are a hive of dry wings.

When you are old
You never know
Whether you live
In the day or the night,
Of half, or both, or neither.

A TALK WITH DEATH

I know you are not a person
I can talk to.
It is to the idea in my head
I address myself
At the age of wonder.

The child is ignorant of it:
He is not allowed to go to funerals;
People in his world simply disappear
        like gophers.

Though elder brother tells him,
It's still just a rumor
Like history, and all those generals,
        and their swords.

When does it become a fact?
I find seventy a good time
For it to loom upon my horizon
With the morning sun.

One can accept it as an equation
For a while: oblivion
May be swallowed like any name
For an experience we cannot have.

Death as an idea begins to displace
The contents of a life;
As a companion begins to bore;
As a solution leaves nothing to be desired.

WILDERNESS

A generation spends forty years
In the wilderness,
Then arrives at the river too late,
And too old, to cross.

The tracks end in a dry wadi,
The idea of a generation
Is doomed like a mirage.

While we stagger in the desert
We have no reserves
To give the young.
We only gasp:
There is a land of wide leaves and peace,
There is a promise,
There is water.

They will not listen now
But we have to tell them:
Do not follow in our footprints,
They lead nowhere.

Only remember for us
There is a land of wide leaves and peace,
There is water;
The promise is to yourself.

TIME IS GOING SOMEWHERE

Time is going somewhere
        without me

As I observe the ant by day,
        the mice by night—

How they attend to everything,

How even their hard breathing
        never bothers;

When they are done, they go,

Another takes their place
        in the ceremony.

I learned from them

To plan on being quiet

At the close of that winter.

Who dares to praise life
        as it goes;

Upon whom to turn the blade
        of anger?

Rage makes a brave poem,
        a neurotic end

adios amigos

THE LAST POEM

Someone has to do it in time
Or only a cone of lava
Will tell we were here
If they come to study the canals.

What can be said in that stanza?
So many farewells we have,
So trite the distraught lovers
Keening in the centuries.

We uttered the pure music,
We sang the defeat of compassion
In the defoliated branches
Of bare forests.

So little spring,
So constant the winters;
For every birth a death,
For every peace a war,
For every poem a murder.

Everything has been said
And we are still arrayed in doubt,
We are going to the very terminus
In the dismay in which we came.

Seal it in a bottle,
Launch it on the nervous sea,
The poem at the end of the world
Is the one that counts.

Excavations (1979)

EXCAVATIONS

I am haunted by the sound of digging
In the buried cities of the world,
By the intent face of the science
Of bones, stones, and feathers.

Vainly the heart of a people
Is sought in the kitchen midden.
It vanishes whether the end comes
As smallpox, or lava flow, or drought,
Or the barbarian riding his stallion
Up the mosaic stairs.

Discover in what artifacts
The boy's love or fear of his father,
The girl diminished by the mother,
The man and the woman in the solitude
Of the stars of the historic night;

Or the exercise of the power
Of the paramount chief,
Or the relation between the entrails
And the beginning of wars
And the drowning of virgins.

It existed for a fragment of time
In an ambience of its own desire.
Who digs in the curious plateau
Releases it forever like myrrh
Escaping with a sigh
The gold coffin of the king.

THE ARCHAEOLOGIST

He has to go away from her
To another time
And a distant place
Where columns have crashed
Like granite trees.

It is simpler to read
A language he does not know
Than to translate her
Into his natural tongue.

He relates to whole dynasties
Through tombs and cooking pots,
Even senses their women
From footprints in the middens.

He needs a Rosetta stone
To enter her remote Egypt.
She keeps disappearing
Like the people of Palenque
Into some night of her own.

It is easier to reconstruct
The dust of strangers
Than to live
With someone you love.

THE CAVE

They explore the labyrinth of art:
The wise, the arrogant,
The terrible closed minds,
The wide open, the wind-scattered.

The secret in the sinuous passage
Stands like a cenotaph
With its stone writing
Between them and the light.

Someone understood in his bones
In the gloom of the cave
On the edge of the ice age:
Brother of trees and cliffs,
Father of creatures,
He drew the Paleolithic horse;
The bison running; the ibex; his fears.

On the walls and ceiling
In brown and red ochre,
In black oxide of manganese,
The experience of his world
Survives the glacier,
The fortunes of history,
The idea of art.

4 A.M.

I try to escape the brutal hour,
I think of those who could be thanked
        by the whole species:
Finders of continents, of newts
        in remote waters;

The man in the wintry marsh
Learning the language
Of the night birds;
Another observing on the mountain,
In the company of frigid stars,
The tidal seasons of the world;

An eye at the end of the lens
Measuring for a generation
The pulse of an undulant cell;
One who lived for three years
With the screams of the baboons
          in the Transvaal;
Also the bones of the historian
Barely left among the middens of the old city.

At 4 A.M.
I never think of generals,
Or even admirals,
Or especially of neutrons.

AUTOBIOGRAPHY

They are calling their childhood
To our attention like a pride of goats,
Offering the contrail of dreams
Instead of the actual nightmare
Of the young.

They believe in the years
With the imaginary mother,
In the iron heroes in the park,
In all their fathers as Paul Bunyan.

Truth is the halfway house of age:
The world did not rise at once,
A marvelous sun in our heads,
Rather it came piece by piece
Like the ceremony of Aztec priests.
Each night was a bony grave,
And dawn came to the mortuary
Like a burglar.

They impress upon us the wonders
Of their childhood
As if they had lived in Eden
With the first forebears,
As if we did not know
Who the serpent was.

DYNAMICS

The little deaths come by stealth
To make the huge one easy,
The way spring hurls its thistle
Into summer, summer into fall.
Winter is only another season,
        the sunless.

We let the child go forever,
The youth in his turn
For the seven wonders of the world;
Yet we age in a day like bees
Instructed by fear of the queen.

It is the same dynamic
From beginning to end
Though we walk in blindness
Among all we see
And hear the notes
But not the music.

We trust the brilliant
Or the complicated of the earth,
Instead of the one we love;
We believe in a hundred heavens
And their multiple thrones
Instead of the burial
In the exquisite calm and final waters.

MORTAL

They say the length of my life
Is in the nature of the veins
Of my ancestors,
Enclosed like a worm in the genes
By people I never knew.

How can I tell the age of their hearts
Who perished in a far-off village
Under a mountain of collapsing lava,
Or lay in the streets of the peninsula
In the year of the plague;
Or how long he would have lasted,
The young forebear, his brain trepanned
By a sword in the foreign war.

O great obscure manifold branches
Of the tree of the family of man,
Where does the artery begin or end
That determines the time?

Mothers, fathers, fallen in seasons
Like leaves and blown over the cold plain
Of that country, did you ever exceed
The grandfathers in their winters?

The answer is not forthcoming from them;
It is on its way with the progress
Of the multiple independently targeted re-entry vehicle
Or its next of kin.

VOYAGES

The sculptor is the fortunate one:
He sees life in the mineral state,
The fallen bird implied in the onyx,
The wet fur of the sea-otter

In the driftwood,
The character of a woman
Forthcoming
From the marble mountain.

The poet cannot use like clay
The white substance
Under his helmet of bone,
Or see in his body, or another,
The skeleton of the great project
Of the dream of words.

He begins with fog and blindness,
Journeys alone on tides that end
On the edges of the known world,
Despairs and mutinies and starves for light,
Sometimes arrives by error and magic in the sail
On the shore of the lost flowers of the Indies.

IN THE CONTINENTS OF THE DARK

In the continents of the dark
The true believers
Are grappling with the cosmos
They were bound to inherit
When their people died
And were buried.

The neophytes are throwing off their vestments,
The partisans of violent creeds are seeking satori,
The monks are burning slowly down like wax.
The smiling and savage gods of east and west
Meet at the meridian where the minds are failing.

After the winter of the death camps,
After the cooling of the furnaces,
After the defoliation of the summer,
Belief in man is waiting to be born,

Replacing bells in their glory
Or segments of bone in the crypts.

The last altar a man abandons
is where his son lies
Undefended from the state.

LISTEN, CHILDREN

Listen, children, to the poetry man:
He never tells you tales
That hang on cliffs by day
Or scream at night like mares.

He sings of the heart and head,
Of the lost Maya, of newfound land,
Of stars and the colored rings of planets,
Of the meaning of the light.

He talks in his sleep,
He walks like a child
Beside the headwaters
Of the river of truth.

He will not pipe you
With his malice
To some enchanted rabbit hole
Down the road from Hamelin.

He will tell you exactly:
The end is curled as a foetus
In the beginning
The arterial clock stops in time.
Listen, children, to the poetry man.

ANCESTORS

I planned to live without ancestors,
To escape the shadow of the dead hand;
In the mottled herd I would be the white unicorn.

They are always there, the old and the great,
Thundering into the future,
Leaving no room for the young
Whose horizon they obscure
With their forest of horns.

Now I invent the forsaken, the ancestors
Lost in the long odyssey of an ego;
I search in the blood for relics of ages,
In the head for the thoughts of the fathers,
In the tribal heart where the songs
Of despair and delight are born.
Cold, I return to the fires
Of the night of the gens.

BIRDS

She believes in birds
And their happiness;
She is a witness to their singing,
She understands chirps.
She is sorry for me.

Their hands are feet,
They have to make a living
With their mouths;
Seeds are always blowing away,
Insects hiding in knot holes,
The worms diving for cover.

The night is devoted to doubt;
Hoping the hawk is asleep,
Hoping not to be caught,
Counting the tiny beat of the heart.

Does she know the birds sing
To conceal themselves
From the birth of thought?
They are eons old
And they can only say:
Look out! look out! the black tiger!

They do not understand themselves,
The others are forever strangers.
Men and birds
Trust in muscles and wings
To take them away from,
Seldom toward.

TRANSIT

I am not drowning, I think,
Even in the emerald riptide of years.
If I were, my whole life
Would be flashing before my eyes.

The fact is: I hardly remember
Any of it, only bizarre scenes
And segments brought to the optic nerve
By a casual word or something déjà vu
Or music of another decade being born,
Fading, expiring, in some lost hour.

I am prepared to examine it
Like an inchworm
As it unwinds in my sleep
Over, say, a thousand and one nights;

Not all at once
Like the last evening of an opera,
Myself the hero
Amid the falling scenery.

Perhaps it is merely a jigsaw puzzle
Whose squirming edges cannot be joined
By living, by hallucination, or by death.
Nonetheless the transit requires us
To see it in that instant,
Laid out like a row of Egyptians.

FLIGHT

The nights conceal themselves
At daybreak
As if they might be overtaken
And exposed with their crimes
And fantasies.

So the stars scatter
In four directions;
The congregations of light
Are running from this globe
Into some other heaven.

They are trying to escape us:
At 186,000 miles a second
They are moving out of the neighborhood,
Abandoning the premises
Where the neutron warhead is charged.

We are gradually left here
In this meager constellation
Like the Indians on the edge
Of the Strait of Magellan:

Of all their tribes
Twenty-seven persons survive
To fish with bone hooks
In the dead waters of their history.

THE OX

The ox moves the stone wheel
On its axis, like a world,
Crushing the grain of that season,
Believing with every step
He is about to go somewhere.

The earth opens to the weather
In the life span of the village,
Seeds fall into place, the rain works,
Food in its hour rises toward the light.

The people share the circular dream
Of the blind ox:
A birth, a death, a copulation;
Wild rice and honey one day,
Or the ribs of a great animal;
A short war and the faces
Of a few strange women, some spears.

There is neither more nor less:
Ideas of change
Have never flown over the dry plain
Like a plague of man-eating birds.

why do we keep thinking of this
in the shaken night of the city

STATUES

Who occupied whole continents
Now sit on iron benches
In the plazas of a hundred lands.
The parts not missing in action
Want to explain themselves
To the young—

Who do not believe in the great valor
Of a year they have not seen:
Old wrecks are always speaking
Of enormous tides
To attract and skewer another generation.

The veins quiver in their temples,
They try to remember
The reason for the war;
Or if victory was confused with defeat;
Or defeat with the music of triumph
In the smoke
Of the splintering forest of guns.

The youth run on their narrow trails
To their own mountains;
The old soldier talks to his shadow
Under the statue of the cavalry.

OF EXCELLENCE

The only pure adoration is of excellence.
There all earthly matins begin
And evensong of the actual world
Concludes in a burst of glory.

The sculptor receives a premonition
Of the dream of art in the stone,
The woodcarver from the tree itself.

They are seen as creatures
Able in particular to induce birth.

The music unheard by the inner
Or the outer ear
Sounds in the depth of a remote cell
In a man responsive to terror and beauty
In the passage of the great planets.

The intimations of the poem
Are moving in and out
Of the cerebral cortex;
Their images stand like the pillars
Of Stonehenge, a statement of faith.

All earthly praise begins in a man
And ends in a museum;
Meanwhile, the human desert
Is filled with light and grace.

SOMETHING FLIES OUT OF THE CELLS

Something flies out of the cells
Where the doomed poets lie;
Something tells it like it is
In the bowels
of the vast nervous amphibious powers.

The nails of broken fingers
Incise graffiti on the walls:
The legend of decades
Of the lions of silence.

When the poets are strangled
At puberty,
Generations live in the undersea
Of the blind.

Even the secret police
Cannot change a fact:
The giant never falls at once
But he always falls,
Wondering why.

The poem has a half-life
Of a thousand years,
The prison returns to sand and lime
While the word flies out of the cells
As a dove
From an ark of the drowned.

THE FAIR COUNTRY

Born on the edges of the Mediterranean,
The dream of a fair country
Moved in the direction of the sun,
Then northward in a cold arc.

The faithful came across seven waters
Until they found the bones of the poets
Buried alive
In blocks of frozen tundra.

Now it hovers in the year
Of the animal
Like a cloud in the mind
Over the cones of blue mountains.

The idea of the landscape never dies.
It goes when the killing begins,
Returns to fill the emptiness of sleep;
Otherwise we rattle,
Dry gourds in the fields of night.

The dream
Is created in one generation
And lost in another;
But the son remembers the father
In time
And with him the boundless land.

PLATEAUS

We have come on the only path
To the plateau of age
Like the sky city of Acoma,
in the distance the great buttes
Of red stone rising as cenotaphs,
Below us the abandoned circle
Of the desert of the world.

All plateaus are the same:
They end in a fall in space;
Memories die on the dunes
Of night; the footprints
Of the ancestors are lost
Like the code in the bird tracks.

We are companions of the height
As we were on the long traverse
of the tribes, in the years
When the obsidian arrows
Flew close to our heads.

Here on the plateau of age
Like the sky city of Acoma
We rest
And wait
In the eye of the hawk.

MISSING PERSON

Thumb curving in the direction
Of the future,
Somebody in blue jeans
Stands at the crossroads
Of an alien world,
Waiting for a progression of strangers
Under the moon of the cool girl.

After a decade of silence
A generation like a catapult
Hurled itself at the walls
Of the empire, the centurions charged,
The young carried away
The broken and their dead
To the burial place of the elephants
Of all the rebellions.

The figure on the highway to somewhere
Does not know who she is:
The child of two generations of war,
The widow of the third.

BICENTENNIAL

How a country can be saddened
As it ages:
It looks into the mirror
Of the two seas endlessly
For itself, and for the footprints
Of its early image on the plains
Of snow; among the clouds
It circles like a condor
Who will never in its life
See the mountain again.

There have been others broken
In the chronicle of conquest,
Also the simple dying of nations
Like the towers of Uxmal;
Sadness too in the faces
Of nomad peoples
Who could not imagine water
In a desert of centuries.

The morning is always astonishing:
The night ends with its oblivion,
The nightmare begins with the light
As the ruins are seen on the skyline
When the turbines of power fall silent.

Hope exists in the time of plenty,
Falters when the mice
Have eaten the grain,
Expires when they stare at us
With the appraising eyes
Of the great carnivora.

THE FOURTH WORLD

exists like the equator,
An imaginary line
In the minds of generations
Bleeding in the first three.

The geography of hope
We learned in childhood
Remains like a firmament
In the bitter skies of age.

The ancestors, each in his time,
Fought under the known flag
Of the birthright of a new world:

Pure, compassionate, the reconciliation
Of all the opposites in armor.

The painted lamb
Grazing beside the lion
In The Peaceable Kingdom
Is nearer than we are, caught
In the iron dens of the destroyers.

The inhabitants of the fourth world
Know one another by signs
And intimations, travel in parallel
On the homicidal globe,
Meet on the borders of the years
As in a future dream.

GULLS

The small dark birds driven inland
By white gulls in the pride
Of the curved talons of possession,
Are kept far from the rich source
Of the kingdom of the shore.

Too busy with patrols, the gulls
Die of exhaustion on the edge
Of the protein-laden depths
In full sight of the next of kin.

They never observe the facets of the sea,
Or the light on the night waters,
The grace of roiling clouds,
The duplicate grace in gray
Of the rising and the falling wave.

The gull exists for the moment:
The pursuit of the enemy bird.

Caught in the metallic net of war,
He is prisoner of the territory,
Lord of all he can frighten.

12:00 NOON

Midday in the city: the congestion
In its chest is fatal;
The legs of the long centipede
Move like a tropism
To the shelter of the daylight bars;
All bodies and metal gears
Are rising to a climax,
A sirocco of fire and ash.

I see a mirage in the noon sky:
Changeless in the Kalahari Desert
Under the suns of fifty thousand years,
Quiet people are gathering locusts.

They are kind as antelopes;
They respect the plants;
They have no wars in a life
As round as the great phase of the moon.

Now in the eye of the meridian
There is a choice of mirages:
The city raging in the time
Of its strangulation;
Or the nomads of the desert,
Content in the dusk of the stone ax.

THE ASSASSIN

He confuses the drowsy world
That dares not exclude him

From the testimony
On the walls of the mind
Of an era.

The contents of the brain
Are observed at the clinic
As the debris of childhood;
The loneliness of the night walker
On a deserted street;
Or the agony of a need to be seen
By someone, to be a discovery
Huge as a submerged continent.

Dreaming in his dark Rome
He severs the head
Of the populace
Like the father of psychosis.

The chosen angel of deliverance,
Believing in his own rituals,
Always knows what to do
While the multitudes mill in doubt
In the great plazas.

The assassin haunts the colonnades
Where the state is dying
In the gloom:
He is not a cause
But an effect.

THE MUSIC

The music is always sad
In the mauve cities of the west.
The young never cry in public:
Exalted by the minor key
    of lamentation

They drift with opaque eyes
Into the streets of night.

The close of childhood
—an instant of glory—
Then the world exposes the end
Coiled in the beginning
As in the first garden.

Someone is implored by the words
They seem to know at birth:
Possession and loss are one,
And life and the coup de grace.

The music is always grieving
As if there is little spring
And less of summer,
Only the cold of autumn
Blowing among the death of leaves.

THE HOLIDAY

It is the day the lonely frogs
Disturb the marsh,
The neuroses bubble to the surface
In alluvial rings.

While the insect is eating
His brother,
The father of the hawk
Dives for his heart,
The wife of the water moccasin
Drowns his mother.

Matriarchs of all species
Lie down in the afternoon
Of despair.
The young seem to escape

Into the myth of the fiesta
But the angel is frowning
At the top of the tree.

It is the age of expectations:
Year by year
The child is said to be coming
With forgiveness.
Meanwhile for the habitants
It is another day of conquest
And defeat,
A long ingestion, family by family.

THE HULL

To be born is the original disaster
In that cold dry white place
With some bastard pounding your back,
The first enemy.

The child survives by accident
The weight of the great mother,
The eye of the father
Coming on like Cyclops.

The youth sails among the girls
On the shores of the antic isles,
Confused when the wind takes him
Across the equator at midnight.

The middle passage opens
Through the gray continent,
A river of storms and visions,
And he is old and on the sea
That has no littoral.

Then he remembers in reverse:
One gave him his first breath;
Two others nourished his second;
A tenderness remains of the lost tropic,
Even of tumult in the river.

Now a hull on a wide Sargasso
he accepts
the beginning
the middle
the end.

THE SHTETL

Born in a shtetl
In the hour of the wolves,
The child lived in a house
Engraved like a time capsule:
Do not open for two thousand years.

He fled across continents,
Still listening for the hoofbeats
Of Cossack horses.
In the cities of the west
The people of the shtetls
Lie awake in the night.

He became my father;
I heard the horses
He gave me in sleep.

The shtetl always exists:
A scene in a glass ball,
The snow falling, falling fast;

Or where something quivers
Like a spent hare
In the minds of generations;

Or there is a sickness
In the pit of the stomach
Of a man
Ten thousand miles away,
A hundred years later,
Today.

THE SEVENTH SENSE

The man who thinks he is a bird
Is in trouble in the world:
The sense of freedom
Is a form of flying;
Someone always tries
To sever wings.

In the country of birds
The hawk is forever hung
On the blue branches of the sky,
Waiting to descend
Upon the happiness of swallows.

The smallest bird
Lives in a habitat of flowers:
—The jay cannot bear such joy—
He has to shred the nest
Before the eggs of spring.

The five senses reach out,
Even the possible sixth,
Weak as tendrils
In a garden of air;

The seventh, the instinct
To be free,
Brings them to life,
The tetrarch to his grave.

AN OLD RADICAL

hears in the winter of neglect
The horses of another summer
Edging his world
Toward an imaginary equinox.

Echoing in the deserted age
of a garden and of sleep,
Recurrent dreams foretell
The saga of the future
Incised in the stony past.

Ascent of theoretical mountains,
Descent into real canyons
Where the jackals waited—
Now quiet of enormous size
In the uninhabited house.

Triumph or disaster or the death
    of brotherhoods
On the field—all are beyond joy
    or regret:
Once in the iron fingers of history
Nothing can ever be taken back.

They are walking to the cemetery
Where they think he lives;
The young, in need of laurels
Or true relics,
Do not see him charging up the slope.

SURVIVAL

He came out of the deep concrete
Like a groundhog
Looking for a warm season.

He had always taken good care
of himself:
As a child he had consumed
his mother.

He walked in the silent city
called debris
On streets of molten glass
And miles of charcoal people.

Everything was his.

The eye of the sun,
Closed by fountains
of dust,
Was the sole witness
To his day of triumph.

a lone rat
limped across the lobby
of the grand hotel

He wanted to tell his heirs
His great scheme
For living through the age
Of the missiles.

IN THE REAL WORLD

Who is always telling us
To live in the real world
Perhaps
Knows where it is.

O firm and permanent as the earth
The one you love in a global moment
With its own space and universe
Until it fades in the galactic distance.

Flowers of forgiveness, a fantasy,
Grew in the earth-filled helmets
After the war;
Nourished by the real world
Of the dead,
They are the bloom on the next war
Just over the burned-out horizon.

Some encounter the creatures
Of their desperate lives
Crawling after them
On the sea-floor of sleep.
The scream is real enough,
The unreal dissolves in light.

Someone is always telling us
To live in that landscape
With its thorny trees
As if we could find it
With five senses.

IN THE HOSPITAL

Falling in the October fear
The old ones
Do not go lightly as leaves,
Yet in the same natural order
To the same end.

There could be a time the earth
Draws us to itself:
A change in gravity, the weight
Of too many years for one aorta
So far from its native ground.

The bone is broken
Or the Isles of Langerhans
Are shaken loose;

Or sometimes we rise again,
Defying a thousand horses.

Everything returns to the horizontal:
The tree in the age of the termite,
The stone women holding up the temple,
The light as it balances
On the knife-edge of evening;
All that is old and almost ready,
All that cannot withstand
The day and the night of the great sirocco.

DAYS

There are days when the earth
Seems unable to move.
The furniture of the universe
Is exactly where it was.
The whole idea of motion
Is jettisoned for twenty-four hours
From the ship of the silent world.

It is like waiting for a coronation,
An interregnum of doubt and terror:
If the heir is an autistic child
They might choose a regent
Fond of fools and scaffolds.

Faith in the sense of direction
Falters and leans in those days
Like the death of trees in the north.
Everything is the same in mauve,
Motionless for imagined eons.
We have to look twice
In the mirror
To see if we are there.

CHILDHOOD

The children are playing with skulls
In the streets of Beirut;
The laughter in the bones
Can be heard as far south
As the Cape of Good Hope
And the outskirts of Soweto.

After a year of automatic gunfire
The empty sockets
Are a diversion,
The teeth are certainly smiling;
After the season of rockets
Anything round or smooth
Can be a part of the game,
Even the head of a possible father.

The black-eyed children are playing with skulls
In the streets of Beirut.
The children on the banks
Of a thousand rivers
Can still, for a while,
Make sailboats of the morning news.

GRAFFITI

The walls of the middle ages
Surround the barrio
Like the stones of a dry moat.

The defiance is stated
In two languages,
In the colors of earth and fire:

Jaguars in the darkening air
Crouch as in a frieze at Tula;

Forlorn the face of the cacique
In the final light;

Later, the blue-eyed homicidal
    horsemen;
Deaths of cities; heads rolling
Like cultures in the arroyos.

Then the alienation appears,
The madness of incomplete lives,
The wild broken abstract clouds:
An undetermined world
inhabited by the nightmares
Of exiled peoples.

In the hour of the sun,
In the hour of the moon,
In the human drought
Can be heard from the walls
El grito de los angeles perdidos.

RETURN OF THE EXILE

It resembles a woodcut of trees
In a country we have not seen:
A woman is walking on the road
Under a black shawl
The color of the death of the men
Thrust into battle by her words
Like an argument of guns in the mountains.

Marching toward the lost capital
Is a generation of ghosts
She cannot forget or remember
Except that they were young
In the year of the visigoths.

In a pause beside the grave,
Doubt rises like a second stone:
Could history have waited
For the terminal act;
Was it just, to send them
Into a future dream?

A child comes out of a house
With a gift of flowers.
The woman begins to plan:
Perhaps they left sons . . .
Or daughters.

THE MUGGING

The old woman was already mugged by life,
Her pension reduced by gentlemen of the committee,
Her bones barely articulate until noon.

The blue check, not to be mutilated, arrived on the third;
But she misunderstood the tempo of the sun,
Walked homeward in the twilight of terror.

The stud was cruising the backwaters of an empty street.
Nothing in the scene in the lamplight recalled his mother,
Or his childhood in the gloom of the unconscious:
It was simply fun and games.

Less an encounter with the grandeur of meteors colliding
Than a tableau in a mortal barrio
In one of Spengler's autumnal cities,
It was even later at the crossroads
Of the winter of a civilization.

KRISTALLNACHT

I was six thousand miles away
When I heard them shatter
The windows of the homes of Jews,
The doors of the prayer houses,
The teeth in their mouths.

Countless as flax in the fields of Dachau,
They could not enter the mind:
It was like trying to swallow
A sea, a desert, a disaster
In another constellation.

I could understand fragments:
A door, a window, the spectacles
Of an old man on his knees
In the filth of the street of heroes.

When the glass was broken
I heard the language of centuries
Telling me what a Jew is
And is not.

Now someone drops a glass:
A knot forms of terror and pity—
It is November 9, 1938,
Kristallnacht—the birth
Of the age of the headsman.

2000

She will be coming of age
In the year two thousand:
A number without content,
A row of zeros indicating space
Or something vast and sunlit.

Where will she live—
In a structure like air,
Like a cloud;
Or in the salt caves
Where the waste is stored
For its half-life.

Who will be there—
One with saurian feet;
Or the prince who always saves
The red-gold child
in the dark forest.

What will she do—
With grace notes,
Or sea-color, or antelope motion;
Or on her knees
In the Buchenwald of that season.

I tell myself: two thousand
Is no more to be feared
Than one.
I tell her:
I would have loved you
if I had lived.

DEADFALLS

I have opened the middens
Of the decades I thought of as mine
So that one child at least might know
The same deadfalls await each generation.

A civilization is not an immaculate conception:
It cannot survive like the agave
In a desert where nothing else has ever existed.
The flowers of Alexandria and Firenze were nourished
In continuity from the Bay of Bengal to the Mediterranean.

Child born under the aegis of a new century,
The horn of time is already sounding
The onset of another thousand years
Of doubt and dream-work.

The counsel is not of despair but of hope:
For those who listen to the insects
Drilling the body in the deadfall;
Who remember the painful excavation of the king;
Who see the warnings rising like fire in water
From the spires of submerged cathedrals.

ROOTLESS

I must have had ancestors
in the history of strangers,
Their names forever unknown.
It is all empty and very quiet,
Lost in antique deserts.

Give me stars and a horizon,
I will devise my own fathers.
Give me the sun and the rain and the river,
I will find a regiment of mothers if I need them.

There are plants continuous in air for years;
Only trees demand deep roots
For their ambitions.
Men can move on the earth
With the animals:
They do not follow in the tracks of forebears.

The triumph is to live in time and place,
To examine the universe
As if it were the first Eden or the last.

GARDENS

The garden in the turmoil
Of the mind of a man
Exerts a total and enormous calm
When it comes to the surface
Like a breathing plant from water to light.

The garden is also composed
At Ryoan-ji near Kyoto:
Of sand in furrows like a sea
And five clusters of rocks,
Noble as sunlit mountains
Placed with care like creation.

A few rocks make a universe
If the mind accepts them:
The faultless arrangement in gray
Compels like a faith.

Ryoan-ji is that great order
We have bled for
Since we crept from the marine world
Toward wings and varicolored eyes
And the mighty chaos of thought.

It is the full statement of peace,
The oasis of stone and sand
Where the tormented animals of compulsion
May come to drink and repose
After the heat of the intense day.

THE MIDDEN

The excavation that will tell us
Takes place in the gray midden
Where the mind was in residence from birth.

The explorer of a buried site
Has to approach it stealthily,
The whorls of the fingers
Sanded like a safecracker.

The man who should be the expert in his own head
Is the last to know what he is looking for
When he accepts the contract.

The historian is armed with a theory of nations,
The paleontologist is at home in the rock strata;
The plain man wanders in a labyrinth of tissue
Where thought begins and ends.

Someone is seeking in this tomb:
He will find it in the ivory boat
Carved for him
On the black river he is waiting for.

THE REFUGE

They go on and on
Like the meaning of forever:
The skinless things in the mind
That never end except by dying.

All day, all day, the brain
Turns on itself, the images
Go round like a water wheel
Run by the river of indecision.

All night, all night, they whir
In the bare silence of bats.
No relief is found in dream:
It is larger and ferocious there
In the manner of those dogs
That never leave us in the dark.

No refuge except in dying;
Even then some friend may linger
In the old house, haunted
By what we did or did not do . . .

As the drowning man held up his hands
For help in the overwhelming sea
While we played some other game
On some other shore.

FREE FALL

I do not have faith in those
Who know who they are:
They have already done
What is never possible.
Like a ship in a doomed port
They are low in the water and lifeless.

I take to those who are mistaken each day,
Whose nightmares occur in the light.
They have few facts but they fly
In the slipstream of undiscovered planets.

I prefer those who go in and out of the psyche.
They enlarge horizons, there are
Two blue lines in their distance.
The chosen are to speak for us all
In re: man's birthright and despair.

May we be delivered
From a nation of burghers
Who know where they are.
Meanwhile I stand with
The free-falling ones
Who believe the parachutes
Will open some day.

THE VISITOR

The bird is out of its mind:
It wants to come in;
It hurls itself at the window
Until it drops on the sill.

You would not have liked it here.
It is not what it seems.
Remember the birth of your children,
The nest that withstood the weight of the wind.

The house of man is moving
Into the bowels of termites;
People are working on a shorter route to annihilation.
Last to go will be what you think is within:
The appearance of overwhelming power.

Lift up your feathers of confusion,
Listen to the hard voices of the inmates,
The Saturday night mayhem,
The Sunday of stupor and sleep,
The Monday of open wounds.

Pity

the creature that wants to leave the sky,
the man who cannot ask it in.

RUINS

The ruins of a future
Not yet born,
Have to be excavated now
Or abandoned to the white ants.

To prevent the last conversation
On the red telephone,
All archaeologists are subject to the draft;
All historians have to be told
They cannot chronicle the great launch,
They have to see that it self-destructs
Before it happens.

There will be no way for a board of inquiry
To sift the debris of a globe
With the half-life of a thousand years
Before it can be touched
By people who will not exist.

A supreme act of imagination is required
To foresee the civilizations
Not yet founded in time;
To hear their columns crumble
In the angular cities;
To strangle a non-future
Now lurking in the barrancas of the night.

THE ARTIFACT

One day the child asked me
If there were middens
Under the waves
As in a mirage or a miracle
In the waters of Egypt.

Perhaps: since there are middens
On the huge shoulders of Peru;
On plateaus like Monte Alban;
Minoan huts sit like swallows
On the cliffs above that inland sea
Where everything great lies drowned.

The archaeologist believes for years
In a city under his feet:
It is there if only in shards.
Someone is always diving in lost depths
As if faith could create one amphora.

So the salt-laden columns
Of every Atlantis
Arise first in the mind.
All submerged continents,
All Utopias,
May yet be found
If hope is the hidden artifact
we seek.

The Sea of Tranquility (1989)

LIONS

The lion in the small shade of summer
Lies with a dry moat between him
And the open mouths of a generation
To whom he is only a mute lord of the fallen.

They do not know he is dreaming of the singing grass,
Of a lean cat fast as the gazelle when hungry,
Resting with blood on his mane
While the young females glide sinuously by.

The children laugh on the other side of the years.
Growing among the crushed beer cans of their fathers,
They cannot imagine the world inside him,
The suns of that continent, the moon of the night of cries.

He sees her tawny eyes upon him in his youth.
He sees again a tumbling pride of sons and daughters.
His mate goes to and fro, to and fro, a living metronome.
She is old but full of grace as on the lost savannah.

CITIZEN BAND

Come in, citizens, non-citizens,
People of the sleeping houses,
Drivers of wrong-way roads.

The wheels are falling off the wagons,
The horses are racing a clock that has stopped,
All interstates end in nightmare cliffs.

Talk now on this frequency before they jam it.
Find out: why everything crawls into dark culverts,
There are no lights on the plain.

The disembodied cargo shifts and bubbles
In the back of the sixteen-wheeler. *What is it?*

The manifest is like the prints of birds,
The shipper is lost in the fog,
The consignee is said to be waiting
On a black corner of the universe.

Come in,
Communicants of the band,
Come in, world—
help!

THE SCIENTIST

He was a refugee from a continent strewn with limbs.
He was at home with infinity and with numbers,
A true believer in peace.

When the great equation flashed like a missile
Across his brain, he stood as on a nova,
Holding the future of all creatures in fee simple.

Did he in that instant see the terror in mankind,
Or know he was Genghis Khan incarnate
Who could not turn back, or would not,
From that slaughter on the plain?

He was a good man,
Not the first
Or last
To let angels die.

LIGHT

I am sitting on a hill in my dotage,
Unwilling to go
Until I see the light of a star
That has not yet begun to travel
In the future of space.

Born in the galaxy of despair,
It will come without a name
Unless it is the star of compassion,
Or tenderness,
One beast to another.

It has to fall a timeless distance:
We need eons to prepare for it
After this savage childhood.
The hostile eye, unable to bear
That incandescence,
Will close in the dark and the dying
Of the angry mind.

It will be in us and around us
Like air and water,
Like a great calm,
Like the embrace
Of the father and mother of the sun.

NO ONE

This street in its trance is a village
In which no one knows anyone else.
The dogs with all their teeth
Are better acquainted than the habitants.

No one gets involved in a scream at 3 A.M.
The armed helicopters roar across the black sky;
No one looks up except the refugees from Asia.

The city is a web of fragile streets like this,
In which no one is actually said to be living.
It is possible to live without knowing the neighbors.

Then why are the cats crying in the night?
Why are the doves mourning in the pepper trees?
Why are the coyotes coming down from the hills?

IN THE CELL

The nameless in a whitewashed cell
Does not really believe he is here.
If he were, he would make friends with the rat—
He dislikes the rat, so he cannot be here.

He also disdains the myth
Of prisoner and guard
In their fearful symbiosis.
His own is sullen as stone.
They hate each other.

He expects to awaken in another place where he really is.
He sees it on the imaginary wall
Like a fine painting of his life by a surrealist.

There is a fifth world of non-persons in airless cells,
Each wondering if the others are there.
They are slowly gaining in numbers on the generals,
And coming out of the paintings into the graven minds of men.

THE CITY

A mind cannot contain a city:
I do not have room for it,
Unlike a star—
Simply a light in a heaven.

A city can almost be endured as a honeycomb,
Cells no larger than a block
Lined with familiar gas lamps.

I have two kinds of neighbors:
Some inhabitants prowl their turf like gophers,
The strangers across the street
Enter and leave their own worlds.

To live and breathe I conjure a remembered plaza,
Its maypole waiting leafless for spring,
Customs observed like a law, costumes
In the childhood of the years.

I multiply by thousands:
Then it is a city
I think
Or a mirage
Or schizophrenia.

MINNOWS

The child is welling up in me,
A terrible fountain of bones;
He forgets as I grow old
The sadness of his infancy.

He seeks once more,
In the body of a person,
A refuge from the perils
Of the light.

He has to be fought
To the last barricade
Or he will take my place
In a dubious world.

Why does he plague me now
Who was lost for decades?
I tried at length to be a man,
I do not need the child
In the hour called wisdom.

We long to die in an order
As stately as ships,
Not nibbled by minnows
Rising to the surface
From their wet grottoes.

IN THE VANGUARD

He is murdered who rages in the vanguard,
Who brings down the onyx columns,
Who numbers the sick hours of the kingdom.

He read the first graffiti on the wall,
Lashed the gold changers from the house of prayer,
Insisted the earth moved around the sun,
Announced the ascent of animals from the salt waters,
Opened the collective to the future of light.

History is the obscure tomb
Of beliefs and bodies destroyed in the vanguard,
Of faith that becomes local fact
In the next generation.

It is the habit of the multitude:
The new and the noble
Must be buried in the middens.
It is the habit of the martyr:
He must live to the very end in his own Masada.

Later: the adoration of his bones.

WORDS AND MUSIC

When the words and the music were blown away,
The young of the world
Cried for three days
At the throat of the cave.

The old were entirely lost in their webs;
The mothers and fathers stared at the graven images
In the mirrors of the abandoned mansions.

Now was seen as an abyss
The black hole in the music,
The crack in the ground
Between us all.

The silence was like an oak dying in winter,
Its mouth nonetheless groping for enzymes—
As even in the brutish season
The air can be alive once more with imaginary birds.

TO THE SURVIVORS

We who have never fought
Cannot feel the battle fatigue.
We think incessantly of Auschwitz,
Who have never heard the sounds in the German night.

We are transfixed at the point
Where civilization disappeared
Between the morning and the evening prayers.

O survivors!
Turn from us: we do not understand your neurosis.
We have our own—the inability to enter it.
Who will relieve you of the aftermath,
Or absolve us of our lasting fault?

Forgive us the human failure,
Forgive the incomplete mind,
Sightless in its fragile nest.

THE MOLE

When we have used the last word and the last thought,
What do we do then for companions of the night?
Contemplation is left, it is true, O mahatma.

Thinking of lost causes alone
Hurls us into another capsule
When they were all alive:
The friends, the compadres, the ones we loved.

We can re-enact the wonders of childhood,
The terrors we cannot forget.
We can witness that distant self, stalking his minotaur
Among the rising trees of his youth.

When we have used all the words
We can at least keep out of the way.
No one will know we are still at work,
Looking for something we never had,
An aging mole in the tunnels of the cerebral cortex.

SOMEONE HAS HEARD

Suddenly I saw the secret in the landscape
From which a generation of compadres had just departed,
Taking with them, I thought, the blueprint of the holy city.
Each who survives sees utopia vanish
With the members of his gens.

◇ ◇ ◇

Someone has heard who did not seem to be listening.
Someone will open the archives on a far-off day of rain,
Enacting the first law: the conservation of dreams.

They will search the bony landscape
Until they find the testament we thought was lost.
Hope is the lever that raised the stones of Easter Island,
That yet may tell them something they did not know.
Why else do they churn the middens of Galilee?

WAITING

Everyone is waiting for lefty
Or godot
Or the orient express
Or the death of the old man
With the gold pesetas.

The general is waiting in the pass
For geronimo,
The carrier for john paul jones
To walk on the water.

Everyone is waiting for ulysses,
The homing pigeon of eternity;
For alice to come out
Of the rabbit hole;
For davy crockett to save the alamo.

Two or three kings are waiting
In this desert
For a child to be born
In the magical year 2000.

Everyone is waiting
For the messiah,
Or the millennium,
Or the missiles.

ON THE BORDER

I remember the hour of dusk in El Paso
When the birds in their thousands
Settled in the trees of the plaza,
Winding their small clocks into sleep.

In the morning they flew over the Rio Grande,
Hoping to find seeds in Mexico,
Or their cousins, or friends of animals.

They had no problem at the border.
They were unarmed and singing
As they soared into the warmth of the wide-open day.

They scatter seeds for others in all countries.
The language of birds, uncoded, is between themselves
Though anyone can listen, even hawks.

Now in the failing northern city
I think of the birds of evening in El Paso,
Their calm arrivals and departures,
Their easy crossing like brothers.

THE MISSILES

Now the general requires us to plan the end.
The brain, after millennia, has at last reached godhead:
The power to create or to destroy it all.

If we cannot believe in our own exit,
How to accept the burial alive
Of the creatures we know,
The loss of the landscape and of birds, of the great constrictor,
The tread of pachyderms in the continents of fire,
The non-being of generations never to be born.

Now we are on the final plateau
With a view in all directions.
We think we can choose any point of the compass
Until we discover we are in Masada, besieged by ourselves.

COMMUNIQUÉ

The music that comes in the night
From the house of the stranger
Is a communiqué from a man or a woman
Who is telling something to the world.
She cannot bring herself to say it.
The music is for one who is listening.

Will he respond?
Will I?
Or hide in the crevice of sleep?
These are the questions the city asks in the night.

Each answers or does not answer in his own way.
Each discovers the secret for himself:
Whatever comes from an unknown house is also a heartbeat.

One is in a room full of grace notes,
One is in a room where they fall.
Each waits for the other,
Drowning alone in a sea of music.

THE DISTANCE TO THE PLANETS

toward which they are rushing
Is the same as the distance
To the interior of the nucleus with its tiny stars.

They are wandering in a labyrinth of ambition.
The recombinant forms are nightmares in their heads,
Pawing the graves of their dreams of glory.

Others are lying in the streets of expiring cities,
Proving the first law of life is death
And the last law to be observed is compassion.

The missiles sleep in their silos.
The missiles move in the waters.
The missiles fly eternally among birds.

Who will save us from those with their hands in the cloud cover,
From those with their forceps in the heart of the atom,
While the earth is blown from its orbit in the mind of man.

ON THE MESA

He is plainly a cliff dweller in his age.
He comes resistant to the edge of the last mesa.
He cannot fly, he does not want to fall.

He sees the ant and the lizard at work.
He does not belong to their clans, he thinks.
What on earth are they doing:
Their footprints go in circles as he did.

The clearest view is from the mesa:
It tells the size of the ant hill,
Of the hole where the lizard dives—
These, like us, are the poor relations of the stars,
On their tiny and pointless errands.

He inquires of the night
Of all the gods,
Is given the same answer
As once the dark watchers of Chaldea.

CHILDHOOD

I wake in a tremor at four in the morning
For the child I do not imagine.
She does not dream of dolls.
She dreams of Hiroshimas.

Her blue eyes cannot focus on the world.
She does not often laugh.
She stares into a distance
Where the city always burns.

Her future perished in the year
She heard the fatal words
And saw the charcoal mounds
And caught the sickness that is fear.

Who will adopt the stepchild of the missiles,
Who will hold her when she shivers,
Who will assure her in the night of the wild horse?

80

Now eighty is creeping over the horizon,
Lighting the long plain through which we have come
As though it were a day and a night, or a breath.

The young barbarians cannot wait to take the city.
They are already an army of occupation.
They lend their children to us like hostages
To see that we do not misplace the family jewels.

They do not know we have been ready for years.
The house has become a graveyard of dried bees,
The ants are working from the roof down.

We will leave it to the creatures who demand nothing.
They drink from the flowers without hurting them,
Their tiny eggs simply open in the wood and they are home.

BLACK HOLE

Each day is consumed in the black hole of night.
We need not scan the earth fault
For the meaning of catastrophe:
It is enough to witness the burial of twenty-four hours.

Everything as beautiful as light
Has its own time of departure
For the starless place
Where there are no beginnings, only ends.

The black hole is an organic part of a continuum:
Pain at this point leaves the body we so cherish;
Even love is known to dissolve in its thin air.
The mind that thinks of it all
Descends until its oxygen fails
In the only heaven we may ever know.

THERE WERE NO PEOPLE

There were no people in my dreams one night.
I knew then my generation had fled.
I was alone on the ice floe.

The more the city grows in numbers,
The lonelier it becomes for those
Who cannot find a face they know
In all that turbulence of bees.

Who once shared whole continents
Cannot bear the narrow township
Where they wait at the crossroads
For the signal that will not change.

Mothers, fathers, friends, lovers,
Have taken up residence in another street that has no name.
Loneliest of all the sorrowful islands, survival is not enough.

NEIGHBORHOOD WATCH

They are waiting for the night visitor
Who comes unseen through the iron grid.
They are praying for the family jewels
Or the sacred white jaguar
Locked in its cave in the dark.

Meanwhile the dehydrated old man
Is dying of loneliness in his house,
The widow next door strangles a cat for the same reason,
The husband and wife in the doomed bungalow
Are on the crumbling edge of mayhem.

A country in love with itself
Cannot regurgitate its worldly goods in time.
It awaits the millennium in the museum
Where the stuffed eagle stares with glassy eyes
Into the lean and ghostly past.

WORLDS

I live in two worlds at a time:
One in my head where the memories
Jostle one another like gravestones.
The other is the disease of kingdoms,
The nervous breakdown of the earth,
The birth of tiny wars in the eye of the nucleus.

At the same moment I see her delight
As the waxen joya comes in the window
And the whole besieged city
Enters the brain with is howitzers.

There is joy in the stature of trees, in the simplicity of light,
And in the red-gold child
And the pure golden child
And in sleep until the dreams come.

Two worlds in the same place
Can only strangle the peace.
One can wake or sleep. One cannot do both at the same time.

THE THEORY

Let us think our way into the theory of annihilation.
It began in the prize-winning minds of the western world,
It grew up in a day in the gardens of Hiroshima.

Now we have to imagine a planet skinned alive,
All houses spent, all trees dissolved,
The lions scattered among the winds
As the cat on the window-sill,
The body of the gray dove picked clean
Like the flowers of the sun,
The bones of the great mammal
Crumbled in the wilderness of the sea.

Who will know where my love is
And the children of her children into infinity,
Their birthright blown to heaven in that cloud.

black sand
black sand—
for this final blessing of the damned
no one can ever reproach us

LOS DESAPARECIDOS

The women of that city are marching
In the streets of indifference,
Holding under the white cloths of mourning
The pictures of the company of the lost,
Crying at the gates of the palacio
Like a field of falling birds:
Dónde están los desaparecidos?

Fathers, brothers, sons, compañeros,
Even the dark-eyed daughters of their lives,
Psychotic habitants of the half-world,
Have drowned in the waters of oblivion.

The faces of the women of that city,
Like the death masks of history,
Are carved in the stone of the homicidal era,
Whispering through their own eternity:
Dónde están los desaparecidos?

THE TEARS

It is easy to cry in childhood, easier in age.
Between the two we bite our lips
And try to walk the continent
Of beauty and of terror
That begins nowhere we know
And nowhere ends that we can see.

The business of those years precludes all tears.
We are in the streets and houses
Where the traffic stops and goes but does not move,
Where the ego wants to be at home but fails.

Everyone is grateful to exist,
No one wishes to be dust.
The tears begin to dry in one exhausted night
That leads to the presence of the sun.

If they excise all pain with their procedure,
If they blow up the morning and the evening, too,
The ghosts alone will weep in that silence.

CHOSEN PEOPLE

They have been killing us inch by inch
For five thousand seven hundred and forty-seven years
That we know of.

Heels dug in the black terrain of time,
A psychosis not yet found in materia medica,
What is to be said of a people that insists upon living,

Conceived on the remote edge of the Mediterranean,
Moving unseen like an equator around the globe,
There is only one holocaust from there to here.

It is not far to the terminus so long desired.
The generals and the Nobel winners are working on Sunday.
If they succeed there will be nothing to it,
The final solution is in the hands of the last gentiles.

THE WIDOWS

The widows of the greater and the lesser wars,
Winding on their paths
Among the fallen trees,
Do not often cry again
After the rivers of salt run dry.

They move as tense as panthers and as grave.
Some nights they dream it was a sin
To give their love to mortals and to live.

They invade with fear the future of the very young
Who hear their tales of death and years
In gardens they have lost but never knew.

The widows are walking in the woods among the fallen trees,
Wondering if it were a crime
To bind their lives with thongs to mortals who are gone.

THE SEA OF TRANQUILITY

is on the moon where no one needs it,
A boundless meadow of dust
Made by a meteor in some dark age of heaven.
Meanwhile, the very words quiet us like sleep.

The name of that sea is required on earth
To untangle the nerves in the streets of the city,
To reduce the cries in the beds of the closed ward,
To open a vast blue placid eye upon the fields of blood.

We have to invent a sea of tranquility in the heartland,
A calm world in a curve of trees, spacious, silent,
Cooling the fevers with a landscape of hope and repose.

Forever in the depths of the black hole of time
Is an idea that seeks to emerge in the light.
We await the second coming: the birth of the great sea.

ON THE LIFE AND WORK OF DON GORDON

Don Gordon was "one of the very best of the revolutionary poets," commented his friend and fellow writer Thomas McGrath.[1] Because McGrath was known to distribute accolades sparingly, such praise carries special weight.

For a long time it was difficult for me to say who Don Gordon was. We started corresponding in 1978, when I began *Quindaro,* a small literary magazine in which some of his poetry appeared.[2] In one issue I published the transcript of a panel on the frontiers of language, which included remarks by McGrath, Meridel LeSueur, Jack Conroy, and Truman Nelson.[3] Responding to the idea of literary conferences in general, Gordon had earlier written me a letter in which he observed that the work was the important thing; all else was irrelevant speculation and theorizing.[4] Here was something essential about this poet who, according to McGrath, wrote in a nearly barren room in his house, stripped to the bones of vision. It was always a pleasure to receive a letter from Gordon because he would so frequently offer a deft insight. For example, the theme for our 1980 Midwest Cultural Conference held in Kansas City was "Creating a Revolutionary Culture"—reminiscent of the old romantic manifestos of writers' congresses fifty years earlier, though much had changed in society since then. Gordon's response: "If the lads would just look behind them, they would see that there is no one there."[5] A thought worth years of meditation.

Gordon rarely read his poetry in public. He didn't make the circuits of the colleges and creative writing programs, didn't have published interviews, and didn't sell many copies of his books. But he did publish his poetry, widely and in a considerable range of magazines, from *Poetry* and *The American Scholar* to modest grassroots projects like *Quindaro.* There was an austere reticence about him that called for respect, as for a laconic master of some ancient Chinese dynasty. Yet he was a friendly and approachable man. If you read his books, you have little choice but to commence thinking. Like Bertolt Brecht, Gordon never flatters his readers, never beguiles us with diversions, but just keeps on flintily firing images squarely between our eyes.

His Life

Don Gordon was born in Bridgeport, Connecticut, on November 21, 1902.[6] His mother, Sarah (called Sadie), had been born in New Milford, where her father was a justice of the peace. His father, Morris, had emigrated from Vilnius, Lithuania, and traveled through the small towns of Connecticut on a horse-drawn dry-goods wagon. Perhaps inspired by the example of his father-in-law, Morris Gordon began studies to become an attorney. In that era, rather than attending a formal school, one could "read the law" to qualify for the profession.

A hint as to the origins of Don Gordon's shy, literary character is that he was born with club feet. His stepdaughter, Tina Gainsboro, recalled that

> Morris read in a newspaper that a European doctor was coming to Chicago to treat a child of the Hormel family, who also had club feet. Morris wrote to the doctor in care of the Hormels in Chicago, and when the doctor was through there, he came to New York City. Morris made an appointment with him and took Don to New York. The doctor operated on Don with a very new and unusual procedure called "bloodless surgery." The bones of the feet were broken and then set and cast so that they would grow in a proper way. It worked and Don could then walk, when he was healed. I think that he must have been about eighteen months old. For many years, to keep the feet from twisting back, he would stand on a platform that forced his ankles in instead of out. While he was standing the proper time each day he had a music stand with a book and read, and read, and read! This probably accounts for his shyness and, sometimes, difficulty with people. He had a whole world in books.

The Gordon family moved to Los Angeles in 1912, after the birth of a daughter, Mildred. Morris Gordon was admitted to the California Bar soon after they arrived. Because Mildred was a pretty child, she got small parts in movies, as did Sadie Gordon, who played New England matronly roles, including one in Charlie Chaplin's *The Floorwalker* (1916).

At that time, Los Angeles was a young, restless, turbulent city exploding with energy and growth, not only in the film industry, but also in agriculture, banking, and housing construction. In spite of boom times, "from 1907 to 1910, a state of war existed in Los Angeles, with the community being torn apart by industrial strife," wrote Carey McWilliams.[7] Among the town's leaders, Harrison Gray Otis dominated in his control of the *Los Angeles Times*. "'By the decision of this one man,'" wrote Irving Stone, "'Los Angeles became immersed in a half century of bloodshed, violence, hatred, class war, oppression, injustice and a destruction of civil liberties which was to turn it into the low spot of American culture and democracy.'"[8] A labor dispute resulted in the bombing of the *Times* offices on October 1, 1910. During the trial that followed, the McNamara brothers suddenly confessed to the crime, resulting in widespread indignation from those who, believing them innocent, had organized support campaigns across the country. In nearby San Diego, fierce "free speech" fights broke out in response to attempts by the Industrial Workers of the World to expand its membership. The noted anarchist orator Emma Goldman was mobbed, and her comrade Ben Reitman was kidnapped by right-wing vigilantes, beaten, and branded with the letters "IWW" on his buttocks. All this unrest contradicted the carefully crafted public relations image of southern California as a peaceful Garden of Eden.

Leading a kind of exodus, the socialist leader Job Harriman went on, with others, to establish a utopian community at Llano del Rio in Antelope Valley, some ninety miles outside the city limits. It attracted a wide range of radicals, reformers, educational theorists, and the like and existed until 1917, when the colonists departed by train for rural Louisiana. Don Gordon's later friend, the architect Gregory Ain, had personal ties to the Llano del Rio experience, as his father had been a member of the colony. Ain long remembered (and disliked) the interminable arguments about which socialist theory was correct.

As a youth, Gordon attended public schools and then Los Angeles High School, graduating in 1919. His high school record earned him a semester of college credits (including in history and German) when he enrolled at the University of California's southern branch, now UCLA. In his two years there, he did best in English, history, and logic. He then transferred to Pomona College, graduating Phi Beta Kappa in 1923. Pomona still had a requirement for chapel attendance, so Gordon brought books to read during the service—from which he was eventually excused after presenting a note from his father pointing out that he was Jewish. "He went to law school at the University of Southern California because he was smart," recalled Gainsboro. "But he hated working in law offices and the courts and judges and lawyers, so he gave up on law and went on to bigger and better nothings." Meaning that he spent the next few years trying to decide what to do with his life. Gordon recalled taking a course from the Palmer School of Writing that included guidance on how to write a love story. It was during this period that he secured a position with the movie studios whereby he was responsible for reading novels for possible selection as film productions.

On November 12, 1927, just before his twenty-fifth birthday, Gordon obtained a passport (listing his occupation as "writer") and sailed for New York City via the

Panama Canal. The poem "Sea," with which his first book of poetry begins, arose from that experience. He recalled that the poem was published in the *New York Herald-Tribune,* but other than that his attempt to make a living as a professional writer did not succeed. He returned to Los Angeles to work in the story departments of the movie studios.

Around 1931, Gordon met an attractive young woman named Henriette Lerfield. She recalled being impressed by how "very polite" he was. He loved to talk and offered to take her to her home, but he didn't have a car. "I loved him deeply, right away," she said. Gordon habitually dressed entirely in black, but Henrie Lerfield soon saw to it that his wardrobe became more stylish. They were married in December 1931, and two years later they moved to Pacific View Drive in the Hollywood Hills area; their rent was just fifteen dollars per month.

The economic cataclysm of the depression years made a deep impression on Gordon. He recalled seeing a small parade with American and Communist flags; this was his introduction to radical politics. "Don worked in a lot of studios," said Gainsboro. "You could work a while, then get laid off and go to another place. Readers were just considered shit! And in the early 1930s, they started to organize, and of course those that were political were in the forefront of the unions. Don worked with the readers, and although he was department head he believed that all workers should be organized. His poetry took on a more political side, and he was *really* an observer of the life and times. The politics of the mid-1930s were just consuming."

"Somehow," Gainsboro noted, "Don was very wise and sage and a good listener. And by this time, he was really into poetry and had stuff published in magazines like *Harper's, The Nation,* and *The New Republic.*" Gainsboro was still a young girl at the time and, like other children, prone to making noise, so her mother would sometimes admonish her to be quiet with the words, "Don has a poem in him."

Around 1932, Gordon joined the Communist Party, and meetings were sometimes held at his house. He stayed away from film celebrities, gravitating instead to the workers in the studios—electricians, technicians, and others who comprised the bulk of the movie industry. Don and Henrie Gordon played a modest but significant role in the long attempt to bring union organization to the world of Hollywood. He also joined the League of American Writers, which aided the antifascist movement.[9] Gordon recalled that a Confederate veteran across the street kept tabs on visitors.

In addition to hosting meetings of rank-and-file workers, the Gordons became part of the artistic community in Los Angeles.[10] The noted architects Rudolph M. Schindler and Gregory Ain, leaders of the modern design revolution, became their close personal friends.[11] Ain was more "political" than Schindler, but both were committed to escaping Victorian models and developing styles that would express the culture of a new technological and progressive era. Ain in particular devoted much of his talent to designing inexpensive yet stylish housing for low- and middle-income families. Los Angeles, wrote Frank Fenton, was "'a city of heretics. . . . It had an air of not belonging to America, though all its motley ways were American. It was a city of refugees from America; it was purely itself in a banishment partly dreamed and partly real. It rested on a crust of earth at the edge of a sea that ended a world.'"[12] In this ferment, there was a definable if rather loosely knit group of radical, more or less left-wing creative artists, poets, and architects who were accomplishing work outside the movies, though, like Gordon, they may have been employed in the film industry.

During World War II, Gordon was too old for the draft, but he did serve local patrol duty in the California State Guard. Henrie Gordon recalled that the guard was "an ignorant bunch"; as a member, Gordon was able to prevent attacks on Japanese people and combat anti-Semitism. He felt that his state guard service was a small contribution to the struggle against fascism in America and abroad.

Because of the U.S.S.R.'s immense sacrifices during World War II, and because it was America's ally in that war, the Communist Party in the United States grew in size and influence. Several prestigious writers and directors, such as John Howard Lawson and Dalton Trumbo, had been or still were in the party; its membership also included hundreds of rank-and-file workers in the movie industry. In October 1943, a Popular Front Writers' Congress drew twelve hundred participants to UCLA, among them Lawson, Trumbo, and other well-known leftists.[13] The front was rather broad in politics; President Franklin D. Roosevelt sent greetings, and the Nobel laureate Thomas Mann addressed the meeting on the topic of the exiled writer's relation to his homeland. It appeared that wartime solidarity between the U.S.S.R. and the Western democracies might lead to an optimistic postwar future.

With the advent of the cold war, however, the atmosphere changed completely. The Left came under attack everywhere in the United States, including Hollywood. The studio heads had a dual purpose in the new anticommunist drive: to "serve the national interest" as outlined by President Harry Truman and to break the strength of the unions. The late 1940s saw several bitter strikes, as well as, shortly thereafter, the hearings of the Un-American Activities Committee of the U.S. House of Representatives (known as HUAC).

The screenwriter Martin Berkeley testified before HUAC in September 1951, naming a large number of people, including Gordon, as members of the Communist

Party.[14] Gordon's name and photograph were published in the newspapers, and on September 24 he appeared before the committee in response to a subpoena. Gainsboro recalled that he sought legal advice from his father. Morris Gordon told his son, "We don't want a stool pigeon in our family," which confirmed the approach Gordon would take in his testimony. The published record begins with his request: "May I say just a word on the question of counsel?" Committee counsel Frank S. Tavenner Jr. responded: "Oh, I beg your pardon. Do you have counsel?" Gordon then stated: "I wanted to say this, if I may. I was present in this room last Friday morning. I heard what seemed to me an improper and shocking attack on another witness's attorney. At that point I felt that the right to have counsel was being invaded and I made up my mind that I could not subject any human being to another such attack, so though I do not waive any rights to counsel, I am here without counsel for that reason."[15] Gordon's friends had been apprehensive when they saw him appear without an attorney, because that often indicated a willingness on the part of witnesses to "cooperate." However, Gordon had decided to appear without an attorney based on what he clearly felt was barbarous behavior on the part of the government. It was also a sign of his own confidence, and conscience, that he chose to go before the committee alone.

Gordon answered a few questions about his place of birth, his work for the studios, and so on, but when Tavenner asked if he had signed a petition to have the Communist Party on the California ballot in 1932, he refused to answer. Tavenner then asked about several poems Gordon had published in the radical magazine *New Masses;* again he refused to answer, claiming the privilege of the Fifth Amendment. He also declined to respond to any questions about people he supposedly knew. Congressman Clyde Doyle then began his part of the questioning by asking if Gordon understood that HUAC had been "directed to investigate subversive propaganda in the United States." "Well," Gordon replied, "I have been sitting here for three and a half days and I ought to have become a little familiar with it; yes, sir." Doyle then stated: "I asked it because I recognize you as a very brilliant gentleman with quite a history of able authorship, and I think a person who could help this committee if you so desire, and I thought perhaps in that particular field you might help us by your considered opinion." Gordon referred again to the abuse of a witness's attorney a few days prior to his own testimony, and Doyle then demanded, "Why don't you come clean like some other men have?"[16] Thirty years later, Henrie Gordon recalled with fierce indignation how Doyle had attacked her decent husband. "'Come clean, Mr. Gordon,'" she repeated angrily, as if the very words were disgraceful.

Gordon was not cited for contempt of Congress, as others had been, but one day shortly after his testimony ended, when he went to work at MGM Studios where he was assistant head of the story department, he found that his desk had been cleared off. He sat there through the morning and then went to see his boss, who had urged him to name just a few names. Gordon's boss gave him his final paycheck, and that was the last day he ever worked in the film industry.[17]

Tom McGrath gave similarly unfriendly testimony before HUAC on April 13, 1953, memorably defying the committee on several grounds, including that it was "illegally engaged in the establishment of a religion of fear." He also proclaimed that "poets have been notorious noncooperators where committees of this sort are concerned. As a traditionalist, I would prefer to take my stand with Marvell, Blake, Shelley, and Garcia Lorca. . . . I do not wish to bring dishonor upon my tribe."[18]

It was exactly during this time that Gordon became part of an informal group of poets whom McGrath later called the "Marsh Street Irregulars," after the place where he was living. McGrath's wife, Alice, recalled: "Of the circle of poets who were familiars, Don Gordon, Edwin Rolfe, and Naomi Replansky were closest to Tom during the Marsh Street years. They were rotten years in political life. But they were also the years of gathering where these and other poets read pieces of poems for the pleasure of hearing them. They were so generous to each other. They enjoyed; they admired; they laughed. Don was not one of the most frequent visitors. Tom insisted that he was the best poet. No names were mentioned for comparison."[19]

Those who participated in this group have come to remember it emotionally as a moment of creative glory. The poet and painter Gene Frumkin wrote that "those days were for some of us, I think, near in temper to that primal academe of Plato. We didn't walk and talk among the trees, but we didn't confine ourselves to the classroom either. . . . It was all a Socratic banquet and the savor of it still remains alive in the buds."[20] In 1957, the poet Alvaro Cardona-Hine met McGrath, who had been fired from Los Angeles State College "by reactionaries sniffing out all radicals and liberals in the schools. . . . I don't know what else he did in those days to keep body and soul together, but the legend of this wonderful teacher and warm human being who went out of his way to help you if he could was already established."[21] Paradoxically, this period of political repression led to intense imaginative labor among a small but talented group of writers for whom the word *solidarity* continued to have meaning. Frumkin recalled how Gordon continued a course in writing begun by Edwin Rolfe at an "alternative" institution, the Sequoia School: "Don's was a terse, no-nonsense gentleness, different from Ed's but no less genuine. I remember him well and have seen him on a few occasions after the course, most memorably when I was one of a crew that Tom rounded up to repaint his [Gordon's] house (this time we used real paint instead of words)."[22]

A literary focus was provided by the *California Quarterly,* launched in the autumn of 1951 at the very moment Gordon was appearing before HUAC.[23] The editorial board consisted of Lawrence Spingarn, Sanora Babb, McGrath, Dolph Sharp, Wilma Shore, and Philip Stevenson. Babb was a midwestern fiction writer whose later book *An Owl on Every Post* (1970) would be widely praised. Stevenson authored a series of novels under the name Lars Lawrence that would be translated and published abroad. The first issue of the *California Quarterly* carried a statement that it was "founded on the conviction that more good writing will come out of the nineteen-fifties than is likely to achieve publication. . . . Contemporary writing is threatened equally by censorship and by obscurantism. . . . We hope to encourage writing that faces up to its time—writers who recognize their responsibility to deal with reality in communicable forms. . . . If we have a claim to newness, it is this moderate position in an immoderate time."[24] Among the contributions to that first issue was a poem by E. P. Thompson, who would become better known as the author of *The Making of the English Working Class* (1963), a classic of twentieth-century historiography. Thompson was probably included by McGrath, who was a close personal friend. As the magazine progressed, other contributors included Boris Pasternak, Ray Bradbury, Meridel LeSueur, and Nelson Algren; the summer 1953 issue was devoted to the controversial film *Salt of the Earth,* which had been suppressed by the federal government. Several issues of the journal also included Gordon's poetry. The *California Quarterly* provided an important West Coast haven for refugees from Joe McCarthy's America.

Another creative effort was launched in the Pacific View Drive house, namely, McGrath's epic poem *Letter to an Imaginary Friend.*

> The poem began one afternoon in 1954 at the house of the poet Don Gordon, in Los Angeles. . . . Some of us used to meet at Gordon's place to read poems at each other, take them apart, talk. Somehow I mentioned a poem I had at the back of my head, a long poem I thought, having to do with something out of my North Dakota childhood, but I had only a hazy notion of what it was about and no idea at all how to begin. I suppose that Don knew instantly that it was more a lack of nerve than anything else that was stopping me. He gave me the obvious advice: Begin and see what happens. I made a beginning that night—in terror, as I have written. It was a more than ordinary terror, which suggested that the poem was going to be long and difficult.[25]

This extraordinary work, published in parts and completed thirty one years later, in 1985, has been called a "tremendous odyssey of sense and spirit" and "the first great poem out of the heart of the American Midwest."[26]

Gordon had many other friends and acquaintances with whom he shared moments of civilization and culture amid the political chaos of the McCarthy era. Among them were the poet Edwin Rolfe, who had fought in the Spanish Civil War, and the writers Cedric Belfrage and Guy Endore. The radical Christian minister Claude Williams, who had had many hair-raising experiences in the South, including a terrible beating in Arkansas, also visited the Gordons.[27] (Tina Gainsboro recalled that he thought Henrie Gordon was "as cute as a mule.")

One day in 1950, while the Hollywood freeway was under construction, Rudolph Schindler was visiting the Gordons when the noise and shock of the excavations knocked down part of the ceiling. Schindler sat down on the spot and made some drawings for remodeling the entire house. Later, Gregory Ain rented a small apartment that was part of the Gordon house and remodeled it in his own style. Thus did the Gordons' house come to be listed in the work of two eminent Los Angeles architects. Both Schindler and Ain encouraged Henrie Gordon's talent for interior decorating, and through their recommendations she obtained substantial work in this field all around the city.

After Gordon was fired from MGM, he was at loose ends for some time. "I'm afraid I sat down and just really didn't know what the hell to do," he remembered. "I was already forty-nine years old, almost fifty. I have to say that my wife knew what to do. She made herself into an interior decorator." He visited Mexico twice and returned to more unemployment and apparent blacklisting. He found work with a mail-order house—"hard physical work for $1.15 an hour. . . . I lasted about six weeks or so." For years Gordon had suffered from awful nightmares and had consulted various psychiatrists about them. Through one of these doctors, he found work as a driver for the Beverly-Compton Day Care Center, where he also helped to administer shock treatments. This developed into a kind of informal role as an assistant and counselor—Gordon was always a sympathetic listener. He reflected later: "I learned a great deal from nurses and doctors and so on. Took naturally to working with sick people. Could relate to them. Could keep myself out of it and learn rather to like the work, the responsibility and so on." He was at the day care center for several years and then worked in a similar role at a halfway house near the Edgemont Hospital in the San Fernando Valley. Gordon later served as a coordinator for the Benjamin Rush Center's night clinic, "where people could come in off the street and be seen for a certain number of visits

Don and Henrie Gordon. Courtesy of Tina Gainsboro.

by professional people." When he reached sixty-two years of age in 1964, Gordon retired. He told an interviewer later: "During this whole period of like ten or fifteen years—ten years, I guess—I didn't write at all. It just did something to the poetry."[28]

Clearly, Gordon's creative energies revived after his "retirement," because he published three substantial collections of poetry in the next twenty years. As I have related, he was an excellent correspondent, but outside of a small, select circle of friends, he did not seek fame other than by sending out his work and always being widely published. Because McGrath kept urging younger writers to seek out his work, Gordon maintained a long-distance audience, as it were.

Although I was entirely ignorant of architecture, when I visited Don and Henrie Gordon in 1986 I was immediately impressed by their home, which somehow connected with what I generally thought of as "California style": large picture windows, modern furniture, and plywood paneling set at an angle. Henrie Gordon told me how Schindler had done all the work, including the tables and chairs. The San Fernando Valley, including one of the movie studios, was visible below, and across the hills you could see the famous HOLLYWOOD sign that Gordon detested. The kitchen window looked out on a close, steep incline, and there was a brilliant green mass of ivy just outside the glass. Gordon's study was exactly as McGrath had described it: plywood walls and desk, a chair, a typewriter (he always used correctable paper), and a woodcut of a forlorn child.

Don and Henrie Gordon were splendid hosts, charming, intelligent, and unrepentant about their political allegiances, though Gordon was not an activist in contemporary causes. In 1994, Alice McGrath remembered Gordon thus: "There certainly cannot be a 'poetic' look, but there is a popular stereotype. Don Gordon, with his neat gray moustache, his neat gray clothes and his gentle, almost self-effacing manner, would never have been taken for the gaudy, outré persona implied by the description 'poet.' I have said elsewhere that Thomas McGrath was a distinguished poet, which means (in the United States) that he was known to seventeen other poets. I would guess that the distinguished poet Don Gordon might have been known by fewer."[29]

It was my impression that for most of his life Gordon was in excellent health. His letters indicated a vigorous mind almost to the end. In the spring of 1989, he received the first copies of his final volume, *The Sea of Tranquility,* as well as the transcript of his interview with the UCLA Oral History Program. Tina Gainsboro sent a copy of the book to me with word that her stepfather had not been well. On June 10, 1989, in his eighty-sixth year, Don Gordon died of congestive heart failure.

His Work

"I had no thought about really becoming a writer," Gordon recalled in 1988.

> I used to write little essays and things, anyway, in school. Did pretty well with them. But no, somewhere in my middle twenties, a girl said to me, 'I don't think of you as a lawyer; I think of you as a writer.' It was like pulling the side of a curtain. Well, of course, that's what I always wanted to do. But the poetry began in a very rudimentary way, and gradually I kept working, working, trying to develop it. But I didn't really know until my middle twenties that I was even concerned about it. . . . I had no thought about poetry up till then. I didn't have that fifteen-year-old poetry-writing period.[30]

By 1927, when Gordon listed his occupation as "writer" on his passport, becoming just that was his goal. New York proved then, as it has so often since, distant and inhospitable to real talent, even though the *Herald-Tribune* published his poem "Sea." It would be nearly impossible to compile Gordon's complete periodical publication record because he sent his work seemingly everywhere. His first book, *Statement,* was published in 1943 when he was forty-one years old. The acknowledgments credit numerous journals for prior publication of poems, among them *New Masses, Prairie Schooner,* and *Poetry. Statement*'s themes are common to books that arose from the experiences of the 1930s: strikes, hunger marches, class struggle, and the shadow of fascism. Its three sections and a two-poem coda ("Decade 5") have thematic and technical similarities to movements in music. Strikingly, the first section is not political in the usual sense at all, though its epigraph should alert us to a certain social context: ". . . other times have sung the rose / we celebrate the thorn." Instead of the traditional rose of medieval romanticism, Gordon acknowledges the significance of the thorn. One is reminded of Hugh MacDiarmid, another radical poet, who set the thistle of his native Scotland against Eliot's hieratic rose.

The first poem, "Sea," begins: "Sea is wild marble waiting a stonecutter's hand, chaos crying for symmetry." The image of the marble and the stonecutter's hand parallels the poet at his task, confronting the challenge of describing with mere words something so turbulent and nonhuman. The tension inherent in a phrase like "wild marble" brings us at once to a halt. Marble is generally thought of as calmly solid and monumental, yet here it is permanently dynamic; the sea is always in flux, yet somehow always the same. Gordon was fascinated by such paradoxes, and they appear time and time again in his work. Nature, like art, continually changes, yet within each painting, within each well-crafted poem, there is a moment of epiphany in which form is permanent. As a philosophical and compassionate observer, the poet confronts and meditates on the dialectical phenomena of change. The "world of man" can be and, indeed, often is a void like the sea, "pendulous, unborn."

In "Sea" and elsewhere in the book, nature is compared to the sphere of human life, and Gordon settles on the challenge of aesthetics as the crucible of his vision. This focus on art is impressive because so much of the era's poetry tended toward the merely rhetorical. This poem compares favorably with other remarkable descriptions of the sea, in Heinrich Heine's poetry or William Carlos Williams's poem "The Yachts." The streaked and mottled texture of Gordon's waves and the harsh drama of the scene are reminiscent more of the American Winslow Homer than, say, J. M. W.

Turner. To commence a first book with such a challenging blend of natural, social, and aesthetic themes is a mark of confidence and artistic maturity. Gordon's poetry tends to hold up so well because it was written not for a moment but for all time. He is always bringing us flat up against an opposite: "Then in salt curves . . . the blue annulment." The "blue" is austere, like something out of Marsden Hartley's work. The terms of the picture are blank realities, akin to much else in modern art: a curve of salt, a blue nothingness, the flat blue of the whole sea.

Other poems in this first section of *Statement* are also concerned with nature. Another "sea poem" is "The Gardens of the Sea," in which Gordon demonstrates his ability to evoke, as in a documentary film, another world, profoundly nonhuman and supposedly totally different from the one we air-breathers inhabit. I say "supposedly" because there may be some ambiguity in the "casual great sea flowers [that] open their languid mouths." Could it be that *people* are like that also? Like Charles Darwin and the other classical natural scientists, Gordon is fascinated with this world's dialectics of creation and destruction as well as its delicate beauty "in emerald and in mauve." His images are visually intense, vivid, and palpable, qualities that many have come to consider typical of good modern poetry.

Other poems in this first section concentrate on the symbolic substance of amber, which is mentioned in "Nocturne" and forms the basis for "Legend of Amber." The latter has a delicacy like that of ancient Chinese poems, to which there is perhaps a reference in the first line: "Desolation falls in the Chinese rain, sorrow is the sound of the wind." The poem's poignant, aching quality evokes Virgil's similar vision of *lachrymae rerum,* "the tears of things." In Gordon's poem, amber is literally the tears of trees. Only through pathology does a substance so preservative of life-forms appear. Again, then, the poet presents a paradox: beauty is fused with death. His image of the amulet on the woman's breast fairly glows. Like the stonecutter of the first poem, Gordon recognizes that the poem itself preserves human memory and possesses the power to freeze within its lines the forms, images, and ideas of all life. "The grace of amber, surpassing light, awaits the compassionate." Words, like amber, can preserve feelings and thoughts that would otherwise be destroyed by the crushing oblivion of time. In "Image of Gold," he says, "I respect the natural tides," yet he sees that the fully human world must present a context of dialectics beyond the natural. "Atoms," he concludes in "Content of the Wind," "have no quick to bare."

The quick is bared in the second section of *Statement,* which includes poems on social and political themes. It begins with "Statement," which, like any other collection's title poem, has a central significance for the whole. Like its contemporary, Brecht's "An die Nachgeboren" (To posterity), this poem celebrates the destructiveness of Gordon's generation of revolutionaries. They could not always see clearly what the new world would be because they were so involved in destroying the old one. The modern scene is sudden and stark: "Life in its marble lines; on his column, God." Humans dwell in an abstract landscape, stripped and bleak, peopled by symbols. Conversely, the people themselves are symbols. This enigmatic and coruscating image of the revolutionary recalls other famous images, such as José Clemente Orozco's *Man of Fire* and David Alfaro Siqueiros's *Portraits of the Bourgeoisie*. The concluding line, "Your cities are at the sea . . . we are the first wave," evokes the sweeping tides of humanity since the French Revolution, a force in the world like those of nature itself: elemental and profound, overwhelming the dying order of the past.

This prefatory poem well prepares us for those that follow. "Pecs" is headed by an explanatory note about twelve hundred striking Hungarian miners in the city of Pecs. From a thematic and technical standpoint, much about this poem is standard for its time: the strike scene, the bitter poverty, the news bulletin, the significance of the victory as an encouragement to workers across the world. Indeed, this evocation of the *atmosphere* of the 1930s remains impressive. But the apparent straightforwardness of the poem should not lull us. For instance, the phrase "their backs sustained the globe" envisions the miners holding the earth up on their very backs, like Atlas. Theirs is literally back-breaking labor, and the claustrophobic scene is etched with concise skill. The cause of these miners, then, is also the cause of all humanity, because they make their stand against savage poverty and exploitation. Another powerful image, "hours ratwise in the groin," could be written only by a poet who fully perceived the unending inner pain of hard labor. The significant, critical details are given in sharp outline: the closeness of the walls, the hunger and desperation of choosing to stay buried alive, men coming out of the crevice alive at the end. "Pecs splintered the decade, fires from below / illumined the dead regions . . . the ruin." The whole horrible and dark decade of the 1930s, as of hell itself, was illuminated by their action as by a light emerging from shadows. In an atmosphere of such desperation, this struggle of the voiceless is heroic. Gordon does not overlook those who are lost, "fallen without whisper at the stone turn." Other similar poems, such as "Unemployed," "Hunger March," and "To the Pickets," are rooted, well formed, and mature in expression. All are fairly typical of 1930s poetry but invariably have interesting artistic qualities as well.

The international context of the times is often brought to the fore in Gordon's poems, as in "Underground, 1935," which evokes the world's battle against fascist masters.

Now imminent on earth the enemy in tunics: hussars have taken the mainlands.
It is the lost season west of the red star but our years
Rumble on caissons—subterrain, the single muscle, the manifold heart.

In this austerely etched scene of symbolic confrontation, the hussars represent a dialectical contrast to the red star in the east. The total militarization of life is heard in the rumbling of the years on caissons. I find Gordon's imagination here parallel to that of such left-wing modernists as Max Ernst, particularly his terrifying 1927 painting *The Horde,* in which inchoate jagged forms dance wildly in a barren landscape. According to Ulrich Bischoff, the painting

> shows a group of fantasy creatures who seem to be forcing their way out of the right-hand side of the picture ("Oh woe, if they are let loose") in front of a bright-blue background. . . . the hordes fight their way aggressively to the outside. . . . In addition to the "wild man" who dominates the right-hand side of the painting, there are also fictitious creatures with claws, teeth, and horns. These hordes and forest pictures were Max Ernst's contribution to the art of the Twenties, as exemplified by the work of Beckmann, Dix and Grosz, which shrewdly anticipated the approach of barbarity and fascism.[31]

Of course, it was not only a matter of anticipation, as the fascists had taken power in Italy by 1927. It seems remarkable that a modest poet in distant Los Angeles was inhabiting the same imaginative world as Ernst.

Gordon's connections to the international currents of modernism and surrealism are more understandable if we consider that, by the early 1930s, he and his wife were close friends with progressive artists and architects, some of whom, like Schindler, had come out of the Central European milieu.[32] Tina Gainsboro pointed out that her parents owned a reproduction of a Miro painting, of which her stepfather was particularly fond. Because of his wife's love of painting, artists, and culture, Gordon was surrounded by an environment that nourished and fleshed out his inner vision.

A key poem in *Statement* is "Testament," an important statement of the poet's objectives and principles. The theme is the role of the poet in the real world, that is, the world of his fellow humans. Yet in Gordon's poem this theme, which was fairly common in the period, has none of the usual hortatory qualities. Indeed, the poem is notable for its quiet and meditative mood:

We slough decades, we the people of words stand unbound in the skull.
We the people of images, being finally of sound mind, forsake ourselves.
In the brief pause of war, hear us creep down the immaculate stairs.

We are breaking the superstructure, the old men fall from our shoulders;
We cleave to the core of our own time, we will yet find the people
Where yesterday and tomorrow open their smoky passes.

A subtle humor is evident: the people of images (i.e., poets) seem to be "finally of sound mind." There is such a weariness in that "finally." When we encounter humor in Gordon's work (and it is not as rare as one might anticipate), it is usually of this kind: dry and sharp, like a skeleton's laughter. Poets act so strangely: creeping down stairways, enduring worms that gnaw their innards, and so on. The image of the ego as tapeworm possesses a kind of aesthetic perfection. That Gordon probably had one of his distinguished contemporaries—T. S. Eliot—in mind is evident from that single resonant word: *hollow.* From the vantage point of a "thousand years," Gordon views the tribe of poets with considerable skepticism. The real source of life is in process itself, where blood flows, like people, in masses.

Thus far, Gordon's poetic themes are similar to those of his contemporary Meridel LeSueur. For instance, her classic short prose account of the 1934 truckers' strike in Minneapolis, "I Was Marching,"[33] begins by marking the distance between herself and the suffering people, a distance that disappears when she gives herself to the literal movement of the demonstrating, marching strikers. But, typically, the last stanza of Gordon's "Testament" perceives that the self that has integrity is critical to creation; the internal sense reveals what is correct and true. It is through participation in life that humans confront and potentially solve dilemmas, but transcending the self is really only the first step in the battle, "the first redoubt."

In "Testament," the theme of solipsism, which appears again and again in Gordon's work, reminds us of Samuel Johnson's statement that the great business of his life was to escape from himself. Gordon often seems to agree, but he adds more positively that we must embrace humankind. In his later work, he often takes this theme further to suggest that the exigencies of survival have merely meant that we often try to escape not only from ourselves but also from everyone else, leading to psychological implosion. The theme is crucial because so much of Western, especially American, civilization in the last two centuries has centered on the individual. Sherwood Anderson once said that Americans were the loneliest people in the world; Gordon intuits this as well, and for most of his life he turned the dark jewel of the self around and around in his imagination. "Testament" presents his conception of the problem in its first, already well-developed form. In other poems, he continues to ponder on it. From "Instant of Light": "The city was in myself, in rage privately muffled" and "The solitary rage with millions henceforth merged: I saw / The core of fire in dust of conflict, core of light in dust of mobile feet." These last lines stand as a motto for the entire section of poems. In "Unemployed," he writes: "The man is in himself, the seed rattles in the house unbroken. // This was a column revolving on the axis of a task." The last line typifies the stark mechanist imagery of much modern art. The horror of the situation is that workers, who are so accustomed to laboring alongside their comrades, are thrown back upon the resources of their uprooted selves.

In "Sargasso," Gordon explores the traditional symbolic image of a sea of decadent lassitude, filled with selfishness and death. In "The Departure," recalling his earlier image of the mouths of the undersea creatures, he writes: "Something has expired in the talking rooms, / On the overstuffed chairs, in mouths nightly open and shut." The poet bids a bitter farewell to the futile world of those such as Eliot who are pinned and wriggling in their tableaus of endless, civilized boredom. There is an edgy quality to Gordon's work on this theme that is quite impressive and obviously of some relevance to the present literary world. "We break from you bodily," he writes, which was true physically as well as in politics, art, and culture.

Most of the poems in the third section are death masks of Hitler, Mussolini, Marx, Lenin, and others whom the poet sets "In the Hall of State," making up a kind of political museum. It is a remarkable technique that brings to bear Gordon's pictorial and descriptive talents. Modern artists from W. B. Yeats to Pablo Picasso and onward have been fascinated by masks: in an age of deceit and alienation, what depths of love and hatred does the human face reveal or conceal? Herman Melville's Ahab cried that if man would strike, he should strike through the mask, and this is Gordon's method also. His first mask is Karl Marx's:

He heard the medieval hound
        snarling for ghostly bones;
                on the rush mat the equal serf.

The new gentlemen
　　　　raged at the cold intruder:
　　　　　　he smelled moats in their towns;
He pointed
　　　　　　to peasants
　　　　　　　　　　in the dank streets;
He said the spinners
　　　　were weaving skeletons, there
　　　　　　would be an end to meekness.

Like Carl Sandburg's "Osawatomie" John Brown, Gordon's Marx is intrepid, relentlessly telling the truth and revealing unpleasant and even horrible facts out of which emerge the imperatives of history. With great concision, the poet summarizes the tattered, decayed, and collapsing *haut monde:* the whole apparatus of gilt cornices, candelabras, and the like. Class society is revealed as predatory, always structured with a terrible logic for the benefit of the rulers, whoever they happen to be. The poor have been the hunted in every age. Contemporary with his friend Heine, who wrote the classic dirge "The Weavers," Marx summoned the archetypal realities of his time and thereby utterly transformed the human perspective. By thoroughly studying the English governmental Blue Books on the horrors of industrialization and by totaling up the cost of a human life from birth to death, Marx prepared both a vast history and an indictment. Even the casual reader of *Das Capital* will be impressed with its encyclopedic range. Gordon, for his part, sees the poetry in this. When he says of Marx that "he smelled moats in their towns," we smell them too. When he says that Marx "in time's bare stone / slit early epitaphs," he evokes the presence of pure vision: a father carving epitaphs for the children he loves. Gordon's command of his subject is shown by his confidence and discipline.

The next poem in the section is a mask of Lenin: "He rose in history's / opaque waters like a delta." Like Marx, there is something in Lenin of the indomitable, the ferocious, the principled. "The moaning colonies / straightened their spines" recalls that it was Lenin who analyzed the impact of imperialism on the poor countries of the world and who insisted on a common struggle with them against the oppressors. In this context, the young Ho Chi Minh went to the peace conference at Versailles after World War I trying to find someone who would recognize Indochina's cause. The statesmen there were not interested and continued to divide up the world among themselves. He was a socialist at the time but found little support among socialists. Only when he heard of Lenin's communists and their forthright endorsement of anticolonial struggles did he find a political home. The Lenin poem concludes:

He caught the first rumble
in the throat of time.
He said: act.
The spectre had bone,
cover, of the living
the steady eyes.

The poet here expresses Lenin's essence, that he was dedicated to action rather than mere theory, and the action of the revolution brought flesh to the spectre foreseen by Marx. The bourgeoisie will always tolerate theorists, but it heaps storms of hatred upon those who act; or, as the Herald remarks in Peter Weiss's play about the French revolutionary Marat: "Talk's cheap; the price of action is colossal."[34]

The next mask is that of Hitler, who presided over a vast charnel house of torture and madness:

The bitter drum
summoned from the Black Forest
the swart, uneasy forms:
In the Brown House . . .
flares . . . fires . . . dead Wotan
seated and blown upon . . .
sated with whips and groans.

The tribal drum sounds forth from the wilds, but underneath the surface swagger of the fascists is a profound insecurity. Though he was and is a dead god, an atavistic Wotan is brought forth to be worshiped. We are reminded of Carl Jung's disturbing 1936 essay "Wotan" (in volume 10 of his *Collected Works*), on the psychology of Germany during the Nazi period, in which he argues that the waves of hysteria and hordes of desperate and often homeless people sweeping across the land resembled some of the ancient myths of Wotan with their elemental chaotic storms thundering out of the forests. It is also important to remember that Carl Orff's choral work *Carmina*

Burana, with its exaltation of the barbarian Middle Ages and its vision of humanity bound to a circling wheel of fortune, also was created during the Nazi period. Gordon probes the inner death of fascism, which is so intimately linked with exterior cruelties: "The skull is outlined / against the closing sky." The legions of the death's head would march over the face of Europe.

The poem about Mussolini is similar:

The taurine head
                    tossed its own youth,
                      in the sour dust gored the debris.
Remained: the angry horns,
          the puffed and sounding nostrils,
                       only the squat image in the eye.

The reference to Mussolini tossing his own youth is based on the fact that *Il Duce,* originally a socialist, had turned against the Left. The image of Mussolini as a mad bull is reminiscent of the bull of Picasso's *Guernica,* which has sometimes been identified with Francisco Franco. The American artist Peter Blume memorably expressed the mayhem of Mussolini's Italy in his large 1937 painting *The Eternal City,* which depicts the dictator as an insane jack-in-the-box glowering among the ruins of the capital. Other contemporary analogs are the parrot-dictator in Siqueiros's *Portrait of the Bourgeoisie* and the angry, thuggish soldiers of the Freikorps depicted by Otto Dix and George Grosz.

"The bound ax, / terrible in the brass parades, / is split at the helve" is a reference to the *fasces,* the ancient symbol of imperial authority after which Mussolini's political movement took its name. Gordon is always alert to the inner meaning of ritual objects and events. Like many other modern artists, he learned his anthropology well and skillfully applies its concepts to the history and folkways of white people. In the throes of decadence and deep economic crisis, the "civilized" world was now committed to cults of head-hunting and torture. In gazing with such clear vision at these horrors, Gordon is squarely among the best of the socially conscious and radical moderns. Fascism was, to take the title of another poem, "The Headsman in Evening Clothes"—while in Hamburg, Germany, a butcher was commissioned to execute prisoners, a story told in fictional form by Arnold Zweig in his great novel *The Axe of Wandsbek* (1947).

In the midst of images of such chaos, madness, and suffering, Gordon includes a poem entitled "The Poet in the Stone House," which begins:

The man is tall in his room,
    his space chosen in the world
        between the ceiling and the floor.
The solitary pharaoh
        cries doom
            from his pyramid.
The people are expected
        to prove his words
            with their lost lives.

McGrath pointed out to me that the poet referred to here is Robinson Jeffers, who was famous in the 1930s for having built by hand his own stone-tower home in Carmel, California. The isolated, reflective poet meditates on the dark course of events in his time. He ponders the sea so intently that he becomes a part of it. He is also part of the stars, though they may already be dead by the time their light reaches his eyes. The tides of history are like those of the sea, repeating endlessly. Jeffers was well known for his pessimistic view of humanity and nature, withdrawn from any political hope or even involvement (hence, "briefly / at the ear of the people"). Gordon later said, "I don't think I was much influenced by anybody, except, perhaps, people like Robinson Jeffers and others who were releasing us from the old forms, so that I never wrote in any form or in very tight rhythms. I wrote more like conversation, much as Jeffers often did or Walt Whitman. But the influence I can't really trace, because I was never much influenced by anybody."[35] In this poem, Gordon comes to terms with Jeffers, with whom he shared a gravity, an introspective nature, and certain philosophical concerns. But Gordon seems to believe, ultimately, that Jeffers's paradigm of the isolated pessimistic elitist cannot serve as a guide for the people.

The last poem in *Statement,* "The Enemy," is somewhat enigmatic, though the beginning is straightforward enough: "The enemy is rich in houses but his spirit lives in the slums of history." Gordon's poems are filled with anonymous or nameless people. Here, he describes a class of people whose lives are mere conformity. The images are rather abstract, but we know they are real, even if some of us choose not to admit it. In this way, the anonymous seems peculiarly personal. The penultimate stanza is:

We need to bear life; to bury the normal corpse; to notice the sun.
We want tomorrow to be constant, to see plain houses built,
Land planted by season, and metals made useful in the cities.

Presenting a rare vision of utopia, the poem is comparable to the line, "After the hardship of the mountains, the hardships of the plains," from Brecht's poem "To My Countrymen," which calls on workers "to take the spade and not the knife."[36] The last stanza of Gordon's poem cries out:

Bring the stretchers! Open the windows of the psychopathic ward!
Take out the advanced cases! Let air pour in upon paranoia in our time!
What we want is order: we will have it.

These lines recall Charles Dickens's *Great Expectations,* in which Pip dramatically throws open the windows of Miss Havisham's closed and moldy room; the wind sweeps the cobwebs away as the light pours in. The transition from the utopian vision of the previous stanza to the image of the chronically ill is quite abrupt and, indeed, heightened by the italics and the uncharacteristic exclamation marks. Gordon calls urgently for the emptying of the madhouse so that the diseased may be brought into the light.

With poems conceived on a wide range of themes and complex ideas, this first book, then, appearing in the middle of World War II, impressively inaugurated Don Gordon's life of writing.

◇ ◇ ◇

Gordon's second book, *Civilian Poems,* was published in 1946 and, as one might guess from the title, is primarily concerned with World War II as seen from the perspective of a compassionate civilian observer—a role that Gordon played in life as a corporal in the California State Guard. Here, Gordon more frequently takes on the mantle of prophet, seer, and "watchman" in the biblical and folkloric sense. The first poem, "The Sealed Train," is about the arrival of Lenin at the Finland Station in 1917: "taller than a hundred divisions, the exile among the dark people" (the latter phrase was a common upper-class expression for the "dangerous classes," i.e., the poor). Lenin's act led in part to the end of World War I, yet humankind later found itself in the midst of a second world war. Though Gordon offers some description of the heroic characters of the new war in "The Black Pilot" and "The Guerrilla," the prevalent mood is one of tender lamentation for the destroyed cities, the dead victims, and the continental chaos of total war.

A typical poem in the collection is "Desert Camp," which begins:

The tents are a statement in geometry, white as pyramids in the moonlight of the
    year.
. . . .
The metallic herd settles in the tank park; only the sentries like slow pendulums
    sever the shadow and the light.
The war is a quiet and terrible nightpiece.

With language such as "a statement in geometry" and "sentries like slow pendulums," Gordon concentrates on the form of the camp; this is a modernist nocturne, made disturbed and uneasy by the presence of the "metallic herd." He often gives us metaphors involving something human transformed into an animal, usually a predator. The great tanks at rest are like buffalo or mastodons.

One of the most impressive poems in this collection is "The Guerrilla": "The quavering earth, the armies on the move, / The solid guns in line, are caught and active in his central points of light." The angularity of the images resembles that of period posters or newsreels during wartime: great lights searching the forests and the skies. The partisan referred to in the title is kin to the anonymous underground workers described in *Statement;* indeed, historically they were sometimes the same individuals. Nature is literally a friend to this man, who knows its every contour and hiding place. The guerrilla thrives on ambush, his tactic above all to hit and run. The effect of the poem is exactly as if the poet were describing a photograph of a partisan: fierce, rugged, determined. He fights not only for himself, his land, and his family but also for the cause of the oppressed in all lands. He and his comrades ("identical men") are the resistance. Stern and stalwart, he is an "outpost in time." His concept of time is deepened by his long family tradition of fighting the oppressors, who are compared to ancient predators: enemies who are so intent on brutality and exploitation that they are animals. The guerrilla's determination summons up the centuries of human history, the burden and hope of civilization itself.

Another poem is strikingly prophetic. "The Antennae" commences:

Midway in war ascending like a rocket, something
is dying and descending, something is being born.

The antennae of the nervous system now respond in
their thinnest fronds.

War destroys the old order, but in a century of total combat, it also begets new and more sensitive weapons. The antennae of radar resemble "fronds"; again, Gordon's metaphorical form is at work, along with the insight that the brain is "the last organ / to believe in change."

"The Warhead," which depicts the V-rockets that bombed England, offers a supremely visionary conclusion:

Direction is plain as a compass needle in the English sky:
Kinship will be thrust upon us; necessity like peace is jet-propelled,
The rocket may teach us to adore the infant in the warhead.

In each rocket's warhead is a dead infant, a prisoner of its potential; the distance between rockets and victims is suddenly telescoped. Those who worship rocket technology often forget the human impact.

Civilian Poems concludes with "Threshold," a haunting elegy that begins:

The mind blacks out at a certain point, only the images of death are lit
In its gallery; the murals we see at night are all of soft surrealist bones;
We study as in sleep the awkward sculpture of the age—the art
Of dismemberment, the separated eyes, the wound acting under sulfa.

Here the museum of *Statement,* with death masks on the walls, has been transformed into a huge charnel house—the panoramas of death are so vast that the mind cannot comprehend them. Any sensitive person must be shaken by such nightmares (perhaps Gordon had these images before him in his sleep) filled with soft bones and scenes of torture as in Max Beckmann's paintings or Ernst's epic *Europe after the Rain.* As Gordon so often says, what we do is really what we are: "The brain is a chart of hidden emplacements."

In other poems in this collection, the wounded recover or stagnate in hospitals; there are vistas of ruined cities; lines of prisoners straggle through a bleak landscape; the corpse of a German soldier is propped up against a tree. Among poets of the World War II era, Gordon here seems closest to the Polish writer Tadeusz Rozewicz—shot through with horror, alienation, and the extremity of death:

It was January the year 1945
In the ditches lay dead soldiers
dead glazed with ice
and the gray-green of their uniforms
was blotched with black blood.[37]

Though the subject matter of *Civilian Poems* may at first appear distant or even dated, its prophetic qualities are relevant in the context of the more recent wars in Vietnam, Central America, and the Persian Gulf. These are not simply war stories; they are stories about humanity. That was the world into which we were born; and it is, to a great extent, where we still live.

◇ ◇ ◇

Gordon's third book, *Displaced Persons,* was published in 1958. Its themes are suggested by the several meanings of the title. After World War II, there were tens of thousands of so-called DPs, their sad and desperate photographs in all the newspapers and magazines. *Displacement* is also a term from Freudian psychology, in which one's real inner motive or the content of a symbol is placed elsewhere—for example, in a dream, a dangerous storm might represent the power of the libido. Finally, *displacement* calls to mind Marxist notions of alienation, including the displacement of a social class, and to Friedrich Engels's idea of false consciousness. In the alienated 1950s, all these meanings were brought together in Gordon's view of American society.

The title poem in the collection offers a rich combination of themes and images:

Barbed wire is the exposed nerve between the war and the peace;
The mice hear them tapping on it the dry monotone of the cage.
The brain in its double grave emits the obscene word: *tomorrow.*

Wired in the half-world, a house in a known land equals their Father's mansion.
Distant artists paint them, ice-hard underfoot the blue plain,
Or in the bare summer with metal thorns on their foreheads.

The first image is vibrant and gripping: barbed wire evokes the displaced refugees. But this barbed wire metaphorically unites the social and the physical; it is an exposed nerve signifying open, flayed tension in the body politic. This is the postwar world with its question of whether there will be other wars and more chaos. The little mice hear people trying to communicate within and among the camps; the two spheres of the brain are entombed in the skull's grave; even to think about tomorrow seems impossible and irrational. As the rest of the poem makes clear, a world so divided by barbed wire, its strands tingling in the wastelands, is also deeply neurotic.

The postwar world is a half-world because it is still obsessed with the haunted memories of the war itself and because too many people remain in the land of dreams, the terrain of the subconscious. Gordon recognizes that artists have depicted this landscape with great accuracy, no matter how bizarre, enigmatic, and abstract their works may at first appear. Details such as the "people" on the blue plain with metal horns on their foreheads evoke Picasso's bleak landscapes and Ernst's metal sculptures. Once again Gordon displays remarkable sensitivity to the prevalent imagery in modern art. His figures are more like insects than people.

The third stanza of "Displaced Persons" takes us further into psychological terrain:

The tetrarchs keep lions to prove their valor,
Enact in the black catharsis their lost selves:
    who search everywhere for their lost mothers;
    who want love and find it in mirrors;
    who are empty and need to be conquerors,
    gendarmes, mercenaries, hunters of pain.

Here is the half-world of the psychoanalytic session: the summoning of dreams, the hauling up of poorly articulated fears and memories like fish from the deep. These are people who are profoundly *displaced:* they cannot find their mothers; the only love they experience is self-love, reflected in mirrors; they have no inner substance and, therefore, project their energies and obsessions outward to the rest of the world, trying to conquer it. They are a decaying and collapsing bourgeoisie, living on symbols instead of food. They are, finally, revealed to be sadistic cannibals who work out their neuroses on the body politic. In sum, Gordon has commenced his vision of the 1950s with a savage indictment, an intimate and unflinching diagnosis of the political and psychological diseases that inflamed the age—a society profoundly dangerous, to itself and to others.

The psychoanalytic theme is explored in several other poems in the collection, including "The Lady on the Chartreuse Couch," who is "looking for herself": "Reality is a drawn shade between the dreamer and the analyst. / The child materializes in the sacred twilight reserved for the unhealthy." Gordon describes the atmosphere of the analytic session and its symbolic qualities, including how the symbols reflect the concept of reality, the half-world of the dream. The original child-form of the patient materializes as if by magic in a "sacred twilight." The poem, which explores the contents of the lady's imagination, its discarded or suppressed thoughts or images, and "the fear of the hairy insect," ends in some cognition of the womb itself and the elemental traumas of birth. In "The Neurotics," Gordon writes, "It was too hard to be strictly alive," and while we may spend our days and nights (that "one third of the time") in search of self and its hidden mysteries, "The burly ones, under our white eyelids, / absconded with a world." While people were obsessed with dreams and nightmares, the ruling class ripped away everything they had. During a period when Freud and his followers were in fashion, Gordon's own outlook became objectively clinical: he dissected Americans' national neuroses with the calm skill of a neurosurgeon. In his poems, as in laboratory slides, we can view in microscopic detail the pathologies of our culture.[38]

Another series of poems in *Displaced Poems* deals with the witch-hunt hysteria and the accompanying phenomena that have taken the name of McCarthyism (though McCarthy is not mentioned in the book). As in his earlier poems, Gordon is focused on the broad social movement of repression. For instance, in "The Silent" he writes: "Now in the empire's lighted arenas / The Romans uncage the man they fear, / Begin the sport of ailing caesars." This is an arena of social and cultural decadence, of political thrill-seeking and intellectual blood sports. In "The Dissenter" we read: "They nail in the hands and feet the bill of attainder" and "They need an enemy to tear apart in the mad season." This form of torture affected the mind, subtly and pervasively terrorizing the populace against the influence of radical or even progressive ideas. In "The Exiles" Gordon writes of actual deportations and imprisonments as well as the inner form of exile that reinforces the mental structures of the established order: "In all conforming tides / Endorsed by the joyful police."

In "Sometime in a Park," the poet describes the old radicals now abandoned, suppressed, and living in isolation:

They carry the flag through the smoke of taverns where the nightmare parrots
 scream;
Or prowl the fog-crazed waterfront after the ships gone down in the brain;
Or sit on the porches of country hotels in the sad towns of the interior.

The problem is that we were all living in those sad towns, buried in our own interiors. Note again the matrix of images dealing with madness: "nightmare parrots," "fog-crazed," "gone down in the brain," "towns of the interior." This poem is quite similar to John Beecher's "Screened," which also tells the story of a blacklisted sailor:

Most mornings you will find him
perched on the ledge beside the library . . . afterwards he takes his daily walk
down the Embarcadero
where the ships are berthed . . . the gold braid screened him off the ships
He asked to hear the charges and was told
the charges were a secret . . . Thirty years at sea were thus
without redress or legal process ended. . . .[39]

Solipsism was the official order of the day, by federal law.

Through it all, Gordon resolutely maintains his sense of integrity. In "The Silent" he concludes:

The man is silent,
His sign of life
The root in the people
Of unworldly wisdom,
His tide sustained unbroken
On Rome's jagged rocks,
His interior sun proceeding
As usual on its path.

The images here are of endurance and unfaltering truth, of belief in those who held to philosophy and culture against decadence. The roots in the people, in the tides, and in the sun remain. Similarly, "The Dissenter" concludes: "The dissenter is born alive on the edges of the weather." The feeling is one of remaining intrepid and still alive out there in the wind. Gordon's image of an "interior sun" is reminiscent of David Riesman's famous concept of a type of person with an internal moral and psychological gyroscope, contrasted with "other-directed" people who function according to externalized radar signals.[40] In the dark 1950s, Gordon found stability and a sense of direction based on his identity and his focus on the truth.

Another group of poems in *Displaced Persons* chronicles the general culture of the so-called silent generation. Recall the subtle connections between this phrase and Spiro Agnew's vaunted "silent majority" of the Nixon presidency. In "Sunday Afternoon" we read:

time floats in the living room
as innocent   as soft   as smoke.
The afternoon bears a litter of musical moments:
Promptly on the hour come in the dogged comedians:
Brass knuckles fix the face of laughter as the murder opens.

The typical 1950s family is watching television in an atmosphere of endless boredom disguised by joyless repetition and exciting action:

The eye rolls like a marble through the colored forest,
The jungle boy whistles for his lion; the ray gun,
The crackle of the comics, recall the heroes lost in space.

Surrealism (the eye rolling like a marble) becomes dull and commonplace; this is a world of alienation and death. The people are still lifes; frozen in electronic entropy, they become indifferent to their own fate. The random violence of television, divorced from thought and history, has prepared them for the end of everything.

I recall very well the day when the first television set was brought to the little town in western Kansas where I grew up in the 1950s. A furniture store downtown had one in its display window. Although the image was fuzzy, like a snowstorm, people gathered on the sidewalk in the evening to watch it, while others slowly drove by in their cars, gazing at the newly arrived god. I felt an involuntary tremor move through my psyche at this invasion, this founding, in a sense, of a new religion. It wasn't long before everyone had a television, of course, and the regular evening ritual was to turn it on. It held my interest for a year or two, but after that it became palpably dull and predictable. Such deficiencies did not appear to bother the majority of the populace, however, who worshiped as eagerly as if it were a new religion.

In Gordon's view, it is not enough to maintain one's personal integrity. Rather, we must ask, What is the quality of life for our fellow citizens? What do they think of this state of affairs? Do they think at all? It is further evidence of the poet's courage that he puts all this into poetic form, which as always ought to include the element of human choice. Other expressions of this view include Ken Kesey's *One Flew Over the Cuckoo's Nest* (1962), which offers a horrible moment when the rebel McMurphy realizes that most of the patients on his asylum ward are there *voluntarily.* Another memorable example is in Mel Brooks's comedic film (and later Broadway play) *The Producers* (1967). In the film, Gene Wilder and Zero Mostel work up an indescribably bad play called *Springtime for Hitler* and produce it on Broadway in expectation of a giant flop (they have concocted a fraud so that when the play fails, they will profit). However, the audience loves the show and they are ruined. A third example is the film *The Dead Zone* (1983), in which the main character has an accident that enables him to have a kind of "future vision." After various episodes in which this strange power is demonstrated, he becomes tangentially involved as an observer in the campaign of a politician for the U.S. Senate. In one attack of "future vision," he foresees that if the politician gets elected to the Senate and later to the presidency, he will blow up the world in a fit of insanity. The peculiar effect in the film is that the candidate is *already* an egomaniac—manifestly dangerous and probably psychotic—yet the people love him, which they prove with flag-waving parades, picnics, speeches, and so on. These are all examples of the profound corruption of civic authority that Gordon confronted during his lifetime. In his poetry he asks, What does one do when the whole society (and not just the ruling class) is shot through with dementia and hypocrisy?

Over the poet and his society looms the shadow of global death. "The Kimono" is based on "the woman in the newsreel, the print of her kimono / Burned in her back." She becomes "the night dream of the spectator, incised on the lidless eye." The woman is present in Gordon's dreams; she lives in his house and will not go away. The delicate bamboo-and-fan pattern was literally X-rayed onto her skin. We are reminded of the eerie fixation of Hans Castorp on the X rays of Clavdia Chauchat in Thomas Mann's *The Magic Mountain* (1924). Mann's novel presents a metaphor of introspection in the context of generalized cultural disease and modern disorder. In Gordon's time, an entire city was X-rayed: ". . . she is now the memorable one." All is connected through the synapses of the nervous system, from the image of the film to nightmares and where we live every day.

Hydrogen bomb tests in the Pacific are the theme of "The Destroyers," and "In the Gaunt Hour" renders useless insane civil defense drills because

as we try to dream
the rocket goes twice around the globe,
the warhead ticks in the bedroom;

as we try to wake
everything is exposed like a death in the family.

This poem's lizards are also found in William Stafford's often reprinted poem "At the Bomb Testing Site." Hart Crane could imagine, in "The River," the telegraph uniting the towns: "Keen instruments strung to a vast precision / Bind town to town and dream to ticking dream."[41] Now it is the weapons that tick, like the ominous clock on the cover of the *Bulletin of the Atomic Scientists*.

When *Displaced Persons* was published, Gordon was fifty-six years old, no longer young, but in the prime of his creative years. He had attained some perspective, as evidenced in "The Middle Passage":

I think of the young, of their disbelief in dying:
Someone who is not there is at once a stranger;
It happens to another generation—always, fortunately.
Willing to slide off the ant-ridden globe.

My mother and father went too often to funerals;
Their lives seemed bleak to be so fond of ceremony.
Later I knew they simply went to say goodbye:
When they were old I saw they had no friends.

The first stanza's insight is common: the young do not believe that they will ever die. Dying is for someone else, for old people. Here, the poet recognizes the epic shifts of generations sliding into oblivion; he comes to know the poignant rituals of the last farewell. In the mid-1950s, the country was obsessed with youth. In the 1960s, the saying was, Don't trust anyone over thirty. It was as if people did not want to grow up; rather, they yearned for infancy and its innocence. "The landmarks, at the middle passage, began to go" and our friends passed on. When Gordon writes of "the poet, his sun blackened in Spain, / Who lived among us by reflection for a time," he is probably referring to his friend Edwin Rolfe:

There are no new words or ways to live with death.
The old ones keep their secret like a cabal.
The ego comes lonely, a recruit to his first battle;
It is not cowardice, it is ignorance about to be shot.

Romanticism is purged; the ignorance of the ego is killed. Mann once remarked, "All individuality is a mistake that death will soon correct."[42] Gordon is a poet of maturity, of wisdom's hard-earned insights. Such qualities, I think, are in large part why his poetry seems to hold up so well.

"Death of the Architect," dedicated to "R.M.S." (probably Rudolph Schindler) notes that the architect had hoped for a "counterpoint to the terrible city" with its Victorian grotesqueries:

He engaged the dark puritan, shattering
The square rooms, the aspects of graves,
Admitting plants and children like pagans
To prove his laughter could defeat, endure.

When I visited the Gordons in Los Angeles, I noticed how Schindler's design of their house broke up the Victorian paradigm of "the dark puritan," bringing in light and plants and children for a flourishing of paganism. "Death of the Architect" is a tribute to a dear friend, but it also evokes the culture of the informal group of radical modernists in California who made a valiant attempt to provide an environment that was progressive, new, and thoroughly human.

In the poem "Someone Always Says," Gordon writes of a typical funeral and of the clichéd utterance, "*it was a merciful release / may I go like that when my time comes.*" He then bitterly observes: "Having said it they are washed of guilt in the oral waters." A hallmark of Gordon's work is that he despises illusions of all kinds, no matter how soothing. The poem concludes:

It is not release or confinement, it is lawful process.
It is not merciful or cruel: it is an end. The human seasons
May not be imposed upon the actual winter of the world.

Gordon does not lapse into mystical visions of some world beyond. Death is an end. Period. He contemplates death with a certain equanimity and resolve, just as he confronts life and its daily march of choices.

In the last poem in the book, "At the Station," the dominant metaphor is the train, a Whitmanesque image for the direction the whole country was taking at the time. Gordon imagines himself to be in a huge, anonymous city's railroad station. The people are woven in cocoons and they sleep like plants, reduced to a vegetative existence.

(Another poem here, "The State," is a fantasy about a man who buys a small carnivorous plant for diversion, but it grows and then devours him, as in the monster movies of the 1950s.) In "At the Station," the people are sleeping; there is a late-night, dreamy atmosphere. The landscape of the 1930s is gone. The threat of fascism is in the air; the scaffolds are being nailed together. "Who has displaced a nation?" the poet asks. "Which way does the big train go? / Traveler, lost under the station lamp, / I am farther from home than you." The conclusion recalls the famous lines of William Blake:

Truly my Satan thou art but a dunce
And dost not know the garment from the man
Every harlot was a virgin once
Nor canst thou ever change Kate into Nan.

Tho thou art worshipd by the Names Divine
Of Jesus and Jehovah: thou art still
The Son of Morn in weary night's decline
The lost traveller's dream under the hill.[43]

In his poetry, Gordon is a traveler searching for the dream. He hasn't found it yet, but he hasn't given up searching; above all, he is still here, conversing face-to-face with us in the station.

Displaced Persons, then, is a volume from the poet's prime, from his full maturity. Ironically, these poems were written in the most desiccated and repressive decade of American history, which only serves to enhance their artistic and political importance as testaments of hope and courage. Gordon's acute sensitivity to the atmosphere of the period, its air of claustrophobia and boredom, of a society gravid with neurotic danger combine to make this book one of the most significant of its era.

◇ ◇ ◇

Gordon's next book, *On the Ward,* was not published until 1977, nineteen years after *Displaced Persons.* The blacklist and mundane labor had exacted their due, yet sometime in the mid-1960s Gordon resumed his craft. Once again, the title poem—"On the Ward, One"—indicates the nature of the whole book:

The quiet time is Saturday night:
the world outside jumps off bridges;

strangles its mates;
or cleans a .22
by emptying it into mother.

We have borders to protect,
voices with exact instruction,
vast electronic systems
wired to the bedsprings.
We have order enough
for a season of chaos.

The first line commences calmly enough, but its suggestion of domestic tranquility is soon reversed. "The world outside" is humanity just beyond the door; the poems in this book evoke a feeling of being besieged by monstrous and murderous people. The offhand tone of the first stanza is effective: violence seems to occur as a kind of afterthought. The second stanza portrays a society burdened with a paranoia that it cannot escape or transcend, ironically leading not to order (as a paranoiac would wish) but to chaos.

In *Displaced Persons,* the poem "UXB" includes the line: "Centuries of unexploded bombs rust in the pale cortex of the mind." Written in 1958, these lines evoke the history of armaments and also perhaps the famous line of Marx's *Eighteenth Brumaire:* "The tradition of all the dead generations weighs like a nightmare on the brain of the living."[44] Almost twenty years later Gordon writes:

The mines erupted in dusty fountains,
the toxic leaves abandoned the dying trees,
the B-52 splattered that sky with the young rice,
their children went off like Roman candles.

This stanza expresses the horror of defoliation and carpet bombing in Vietnam. Gordon's asperities are superbly chiseled, with tension between extreme violence and the disciplined concision of a line: "their children went off like Roman candles." The earth, trees, rice, and children are all ripped apart by humankind's weapons. Gordon powerfully expresses the intricate connection between what we producc and what we see around us, between what we are and what we think. He sees this in

Marxist terms of the relationship among society, social classes, technology, and the "superstructure" of ideas and culture. For Gordon, unlike many political poets, these relationships are not economically determined but dialectical.

Many poems in this book present a world of demented violence: murder, street attacks, suicide, burning monks, hunting, dismemberment, defoliation, and genocide. The predominance of this theme might suggest that the poet is somehow obsessed, yet our overall impression of the collection is the opposite. Gordon writes from a perspective of health. In his work there is nothing of Eliot's secret complicity and final divergence into religious mysticism. Gordon's own vision is fiercely clear, though it increasingly seems to him less likely to prevail. Often what he confronts is almost unbearably painful, as in "On the Ward, Two":

In all religions the mad are sacred;

We bear the sign from the godhead
        like the entrails of birds.

We are not about to tell them
        the truth:

The only bomb shelter is psychosis.

Out of atavistic sacrifices emerge the modern forms of madness, or what we define as psychosis. The poet's tone is of meditative sadness, like a physician coming to a firm but undeniable diagnosis of terminal disease. It seems likely that Gordon's years of personal interaction with the mentally ill provided a wealth of experience in this regard. He had been, literally, "on the ward."

In Gordon's poems, vast impersonal forces surge through the world, seizing us in an irrational embrace. In "Killing," the theme is distance:

At thirty thousand feet
There are no dimensions:
The Himalayan dust you make
Obscures the marionettes
Sliding in the river.

These lines reveal the point of view of the American pilots in Vietnam who rarely saw the peasants they destroyed: the people are only mechanical dolls, sliding with horrible ease into the river. This poem brings out the alienation of modern life, the simple distance we maintain from each other. We do not perceive who others are or even who we are. In "They Could Not Lift Their Heads," the ancient Irish elks grow horns so large and elaborate that the elks become immobile and perish:

Whole lives are said to perish
In the exhausting civil war
Between fact and fantasy.
Nations fall into grief and despair
As the armies of the lemmings
Hurry on fur-covered feet
To drown in northern waters.

Divided among ourselves, we revert to a former stage of existence, to a purely feral world. The same theme of evolution's lessons was developed to great effect in Thomas McGrath's poem "Ode for the American Dead in Asia" in the lines: "No scholar put your thinking cap on nor / Warned that in dead seas fish died in schools / Before inventing legs to walk the land."[45] The neglect of science in American education is now a common lament, but these two radical poets clearly foresaw its social consequences more than forty years ago.

In his later books, Gordon often portrays America's urban environment as what Mike Davis has called "today's pharaonic scales of residential and commercial security" that make up "'fortress cities' brutally divided between 'fortified cells' of affluent society and 'places of terror' where the police battle the criminalized poor."[46] Davis documents how southern California pioneered such innovations, walling people off from each other. I remember once, past the exit of a UCLA parking lot, seeing a sign warning, "Danger: Tire Damage." Sharp spikes, protruding from a steel grate mounted in the road, seemed like something out of the Middle Ages (their purpose, of course, was to discourage drivers from entering that exit). In his poems, Gordon articulates this dark underside of the so-called American Dream.

The poet finds signs of hope, however, in the civil rights struggle. "The Child" begins:

Deep as a mole,
In the night world I lie,
Buried to the eyeball
In thoughts of violence.

This stanza reveals the locale of poetry's origins for Gordon: the subterranean, surrealist world of nightmares. Then he remembers a scene:

The school is ringed by guns;
Through snake sound and spittle,
Through the cottonmouth women
I see the black child go.

The small black child makes her way into a segregated school. One is reminded of Robert Lowell's poem "For the Union Dead": "When I crouch to my television set, / the drained faces of Negro school-children rise like balloons."[47] Gordon finds inspiration in this tiny act of courage:

Child of love,
Child of an act of faith!
To this light
Even the blind mole may come.

The child's light, a moral beacon in the American gloom, could attract and illuminate even the blind mole, meaning the people of America.

Another poem, "The Underground Railroad," recalls the ancestors of the civil rights movement. The poet connects contemporary actions with those of previous generations:

He went down
at the edge
of the cane-brake,

slept with animals

came up in the latitude
of dissenters.

The landmarks of those journeys are needed again.

There is a visceral feeling in the lines about coming up in the latitude of dissenters. It is necessary to surface for air in the land of the intellectually free. Here, the underground railroad is really a passage for all those who seek liberty and justice, a "passage for ideas."

The problem is, Gordon says, that the circumstances of the world are so terrible that, in the words of the poem's title, "We Are Not Ready":

    for the collective:
It requires a state of grace
Light years from these war cries
On the violent desert.

The people of the mind
Live in its cerebral caves:
When the door opens
On the real world
They hear the nightriding mares.

This poem explores society's distance from utopia; the creators ("people of the mind") are too obsessed with their own worlds and can scarcely see any way out. Gordon writes:

We sleep and imagine the landscape
Of the commune in its glory
Rising with each century
And dying with it.

This dedication to the "commune" is another link between Gordon and McGrath, who dedicated his *Letter to an Imaginary Friend* to the "Commune." In part, the word preserves the memory of the great, tragic Paris Commune of 1871; but beyond that, it evokes the age-old idea of utopia, a society that would be based on justice and equality. But, says Gordon, "It demands more than a belief / In our sleep / To enter the peaceable kingdom." That is, it will require conscious, organized effort and a vision of what that land could be. The utopian commune can never be attained by those trapped in merely "cerebral caves."

On the Ward concludes with a series of poems about aging, though to label them so is like saying Shakespeare's *King Lear* is a play about senility. In "Neolithic," Gordon writes:

I am turning to stone:
I feel the calcium
Adhere to the spine,
The stalagmites rising
From my feet,
The stalactites growing down
From my brain;
When they meet in my chest
Like the teeth of rodents
I will know it is time.

These lines describe the slow but certain calcification of the arteries; the body is likened to a cave in which limestone formations resemble teeth. There is a link and a tension between the slow process of calcification and the sudden heart attack. The rest of the poem develops a metaphor of the poet as a wounded bull who lurches in circles. Gordon contemplates his infirmities and approaching dissolution with a gentle sense of humor. The title is instructive: this is a stone age, and the aged poet is turning to stone. In Gordon's work, stone is the blank, nonhuman aspect of nature and the cosmos. When we become stone, we physically revert to inanimate nature.

"The Contract" contemplates the poet's body, "given . . . to science." Gordon writes, "Under a bank of florescent suns / The people with knives / . . . / . . . are going to look for me." Surely it is unusual for a poet to contemplate with such equanimity his physical and poetic dissection, the last vestiges of Romanticism stripped away. The poem is a testament to Gordon's belief in science, but it also reveals a tender sense of acceptance and even humor. Somewhere in his brain are convolutions "pointing to some obscure trouble"—a huge understatement for a poet fixed on the great epic catastrophes of the twentieth century. At this point his tone is almost serene, though he counts himself among those who search for "light / Among the tangled ropes of darkness." His actual self will dissipate with the end of his life because his body is only a kind of husk. For a poet who in life was shy and almost reclusive, such an end seems especially fitting. One wonders whether some future explicator of Gordon's verbal corpus is not included in the circle of eager students with knives?[48]

On the Ward proceeds from an assumption of social and public sickness that appears to be terminal, through a few signs of hope in the momentum of the civil rights movement and in cultural memories of utopia, to the prospect of personal aging, illness, and death. The poet comes to accept this inevitability with a new sense of calm and a wry but tender sense of humor. Lorca wrote that poets travel to the country of inspiration but always return to reflect on and shape what they have discovered. In this collection Gordon has gone to that country and found out that, like the real world, it is preoccupied with terror, war, and survival. He gazes steadily at something almost uncontrolled—hence the metaphor of the ward—and manages to retain his sanity and his control. He does not hesitate to use emotive language—the heart is a prevalent image—but he always preserves his reason with an iron will. He does not flinch at declaring the order of things in America to be mostly insane, but, unlike many other poets, he detests such a state of affairs and indicates a door leading out of it all—an escape from the prison of the self.

◇ ◇ ◇

Gordon's fifth book, dated 1979, was released in the spring of 1980, just three years after *On the Ward,* while he was in his seventy-eighth year. Entitled *Excavations,* its poems are for the most part a kind of cultural anthropology for his time, philosophical and reflective, as much preoccupied with death and burial as the previous book was concerned with sickness. The title poem begins:

I am haunted by the sound of digging
In the buried cities of the world,
By the intent face of the science
Of bones, stones, and feathers.

A key image that recurs throughout the collection is "midden"—a refuse heap, especially a mound that marks the site of primitive human habitation. I have noted Gordon's long-time interest in anthropology and how he applied the ideas and concepts of that field to white people. Here, as he contemplates his own end, he meditates on the meaning of human society at a time when it is facing complete extinction through a nuclear threat. Life—the way people dream and fear—cannot be discerned from material artifacts, and in these poems are a new sense of life's evanescence, its fragile and fragmentary qualities. Gordon ponders not so much the class struggle, neurosis, and political repression as the nature of the world and the human condition. He has surrendered none of his evocative powers, as evidenced by the "ambience of its own desire" in an ancient society that, when the archaeologist digs, he releases, "forever like myrrh / Escaping with a sigh / The gold coffin of the king." Perhaps poetry, too, is as elusive and fleeting as myrrh.

Other poems in this collection continue Gordon's search for elemental human meanings. "Ancestors" reveals that the poet, in his youth, had been rather uninterested in his forebears; he had thought of himself romantically as a "white unicorn" in the "mottled herd." Now older and wiser, he invents "the forsaken, the ancestors / Lost in the long odyssey of an ego" and concludes: "Cold, I return to the fires / Of the night of the gens." Don and Henrie Gordon had once taken a cross-country vacation by car, and one of the places they visited was the great plateau of the Acomas in New Mexico, which, in "Plateau," becomes a symbol of humankind's endurance:

All plateaus are the same:
They end in a fall in space;
Memories die on the dunes
Of night; the footprints
Of the ancestors are lost
Like the code in the bird tracks.

In spite of such departures, not to be reclaimed or ever fully understood, Gordon is never indifferent; on the contrary, his sense of compassion is deepened yet further. Another poem in *Excavations* is entitled "Ruins"; the final one is "The Artifact." Developing from a first mention of "midden" in *Displaced Persons* (in "The Dissenter": "People will turn the middens we bequeath"), Gordon reaffirms his ties with the common heritage of humankind.

The poet also pursues his idea of art as a important means of preserving something vital about human culture. "The Cave" evokes the archetypal cave paintings of prehistoric Europeans:

The secret in the sinuous passage
Stands like a cenotaph

With its stone writing
Between them and the light.

In another poem, "Of Excellence," he suggests the process of creation itself in a powerful image:

The intimations of the poem
Are moving in and out
Of the cerebral cortex;
Their images stand like the pillars
Of Stonehenge, a statement of faith.

Gordon's images are craggy and weathered in their endurance and strength and in their meaning as gray rubrics of eternity. He often uses the image of stone as a symbol of the nonhuman, of the permanent, of mute nature; in these poems, his own images have all the lasting qualities of stone. His is a proud vision expressed in rare elegiac music, a victory not to be denied a poet who has earned it by surviving and by continuing to hew his work out of the world's raw matter. His cortex has become one with the earth.

The poem "Voyages" may be an homage to Charles Baudelaire, who wrote a poem with the same title and the same metaphorical description of the creative process as departing on a voyage. In Gordon's poem, the sculptor is fortunate compared to the poet, who

. . . begins with fog and blindness,
Journeys alone on tides that end
On the edges of the known world,
Despairs and mutinies and starves for light,
Sometimes arrives by error and magic in the sail
On the shore of the lost flowers of the Indies.

These lines are comparable to Baudelaire's:

Amazing travellers, what noble stories
We read in the deep oceans of your gaze!

Show us your memory's casket, and the glories
Streaming from gems made out of stars and rays![49]

In a sense, Gordon's poem is a return to the sea, that marine world of the first poem of his first book, but also with reference to the sculptor and the "wild marble" of the waves. This poem is a meditation on the special technical difficulties that writers face: they must, as it were, shape their creations out of thin air—that is, out of words—rather than out of tangible substances such as wood or marble. Gordon also continues the anatomical metaphors of his previous book, referring to the "white substance" (his brain) like clay, "under his helmet of bone." Throughout his work, Gordon maintains a consistent and nondogmatic materialist approach to life: thoughts, desires, ideas, and social conflicts all arise from bodily existence. According to Baudelaire, "The true voyagers are those who depart in order to depart."[50] Gordon expresses a similar idea in writing of leaving known continents in a kind of wild desperation and thirst for discovery. For him, there is always the promise or hope of a new world waiting at the end of the journey.

In his later books, Gordon wanted to leave a record of his principles and his vision for humanity. "Free Fall" tells us:

I take to those who are mistaken each day,
Whose nightmares occur in the light.
They have few facts but they fly
In the slipstream of undiscovered planets.

His years of experience with the mentally ill, particularly his time at the walk-in free clinic, are here brought to bear. He told the UCLA oral history interviewer in 1988 that he felt a kinship with these patients, who did not dissemble their predicament: they knew planets other than Earth. "I prefer those who go in and out of the psyche," he continues in "Free Fall." "They enlarge horizons, there are / Two blue lines in their distance." The sharp, angular, visual detail is as clear as a painting, and as stark.

May we be delivered
From a nation of burghers
Who know where they are.
Meanwhile I stand with

The free-falling ones
Who believe the parachutes
Will open some day.

Those who create must be ready for difficulties, danger, doubt, and despair, not cynically or due to religious conversion (like T. S. Eliot), but because art must take the side of life, especially of those on the edge. The disdainful reference to "burghers" ranks Gordon still with the antibourgeoisie. He has no love for the merely respectable, for the delivery of received wisdom, or for mumbled platitudinous litanies.

A number of poems in *Excavations* express a kinship with the life of animals, especially birds: "Birds," "Gulls," "Flight," and "Something Flies Out of the Cells." In the latter, poems fly out of the cells of the doomed poets, who are prisoners of humankind's imagination. In "The Seventh Sense," Gordon again pursues the image of the individual and flight:

The man who thinks he is a bird
Is in trouble with the world:
The sense of freedom
Is a form of flying;
Someone always tries
To sever wings.

The bird is a traditional symbol for the imagination; the dove of the Christian gospels is the Holy Spirit. In ancient mythology, Daedalus tried to fly up to the sun and perished. Freud believed that flying was an expression of libidinal energy. The patients Gordon counseled no doubt had such fantasies, but he recognizes that these people are "in trouble in the world" and that the world also wants to sever their wings, to repress and control their desires.

That the poet never surrendered his principles is evident in "An Old Radical," who

hears in the winter of neglect
The horses of another summer
Edging his world
Toward an imaginary equinox.

Henrie and Don Gordon, with Alice and Thomas McGrath, 1984. Courtesy of the photographer, John Crawford.

Through "recurrent dreams" and the "ascent of theoretical mountains," he arrives at an epiphany:

Triumph or disaster or the death
        of brotherhoods
On the field—all are beyond joy
        or regret:
Once in the iron fingers of history
Nothing can ever be taken back.

They are walking to the cemetery
Where they think he lives;
The young, in need of laurels
Or true relics,
Do not see him charging up the slope.

Gordon lived through many winters of neglect; here, in these poems of old age, he slips into a reflective mode of thought. There have been so many defeats, losses, and disasters on the battlefields, resulting in "the death of brotherhoods," yet age and experience have allowed him to come to terms with time and history, whose iron fingers have a remorseless grip. The young may seek him out with laurels of fame, trying to find the true relics of a literary religion, but he is far ahead of them, confronting the enemy.

◇ ◇ ◇

Gordon's sixth and final volume, *The Sea of Tranquility,* appeared in the spring of 1989. It serves as a coda to the main body of his work, rather like Beethoven's last string quartets. Its thirty-one poems concentrate on a theme familiar to Gordon's readers by this point: the continuing chaos and decline of American society in terms of alienation and violence ("Citizen Band," "The City," etc.). There are also poems on the negative aspects of modern science and technology. "The Missiles" returns to the threat of nuclear annihilation; "The Scientist" is a portrait of Albert Einstein: "When the great equation flashed like a missile / Across his brain, he stood as on a nova." Scientific innovations have exceeded all rational control—even the pleas of those who developed them: ". . . he was Genghis Khan incarnate."

In "Lions," the poet imagines himself as an aged animal patriarch: "His mate goes to and fro, to and fro, a living metronome. / She is old but full of grace as on the lost savannah." Other animal images are of bees ("The house has become a graveyard of dried bees" ["80"]), moles ("An aging mole in the tunnels of the cerebral cortex" ["The Mole"]), and spiders ("The old were entirely lost in their webs" ["Words and Music"]). These poems portray old age as a time of decline and desiccation; humans, like all animals, are inevitably prey to the course of nature. The young scarcely know that the old exist. The vantage point is of "sitting on a hill in my dotage" ("Light"), and there are similar references to being on a mesa or on Masada, the famous plateau in Israel where a small fugitive band of Jews first held off the Roman army and then committed collective suicide rather than surrender. Gordon feels isolated, but he can see farther than others. One of the most moving poems in this collection is "On the Border," in which he recalls seeing thousands of birds settling on the trees in El Paso's plaza; they fly back and forth at will between the United States and Mexico and "scatter seeds for others in all countries":

Now in the failing northern city
I think of the birds of evening in El Paso,
Their calm arrivals and departures,
Their easy crossing like brothers.

This "nature" poem reveals an understanding that the world knows no national boundaries: they are merely artificial human inventions.

In *The Sea of Tranquility,* Gordon seems also to arrive at a final understanding of his own character and personal demons. He returns to his theme of nightmares: "I wake in a tremor at four in the morning" ("Childhood") and "There were no people in my dreams one night" ("There Were No People"). He thinks of himself as a prisoner who

. . . expects to awaken in another place where he really is.
He sees it on the imaginary wall
Like a fine painting of his life by a surrealist. ("In the Cell")

The reference to surrealism suggests its continuing importance in Gordon's imaginative world. "Worlds" is a retrospective on an entire life:

I live in two worlds at a time:
One in my head where the memories
Jostle one another like gravestones.
The other is the disease of kingdoms,
The nervous breakdown of the earth,
The birth of tiny wars in the eye of the nucleus.

For decades, Gordon straddled the dialectic between his own personal obsessions—a certain preoccupation with death ("gravestones")—and the death of the world, in which the earth itself seems to be having a nervous breakdown. In "Worlds" he offers a lovely reference to Henrie Gordon as a counterpoint to chaos: "At the same moment I see her delight / As the waxen joya comes in the window." The Gordon house was surrounded by century plants, joya trees, and all manner of flowers. Henrie Gordon had preserved some remnant of paradise in the middle of the city's mayhem: "There is joy in the stature of trees, in the simplicity of light." The last paintings of the artist Peter Blume, who had similar political and surreal experiences, have this same peaceful, almost idyllic quality.[51]

Gordon's last collection is his most existential; his perspective becomes planetary, like Max Ernst's in his final paintings. There are poems that focus on elemental realities, such as "Light," in which the poet longs to "see the light of a star / That has not yet begun to travel / In the future of space." He continues:

Born in the galaxy of despair,
It will come without a name
Unless it is the star of compassion,
Or tenderness,
One beast to another.

These lines seem to prophesy a new form of society, for life and consciousness, not so much ideological as arising from the fundamentals of existence itself:

It will be in us and around us
Like air and water,
Like a great calm,
Like the embrace
Of the father and mother of the sun.

Other poems in *The Sea of Tranquility* explore the astral theme: black holes become complex symbols, a vacuum at the core of individual beings or, perhaps, sites of personal dissolution in "the starless place / Where there are no beginnings, only ends" ("Black Hole"). All who love life regret leaving it, but philosophy teaches us that this is the course of nature.

The final poem in the volume and of the poet's life is the title poem, "The Sea of Tranquility," which "is on the moon where no one needs it." Its name is "required on earth / To untangle the nerves in the streets of the city." We need calm to deal with the "cries in the beds of the closed ward"—an allusion to Gordon's years assisting in the care of the mentally ill. But then he writes,

We have to invent a sea of tranquility in the heartland,
A calm world in a curve of trees, spacious, silent,
Cooling the fevers with a landscape of hope and repose.

There are no saints or angels in this heaven; it is wholly of the earth, a place of peace at last. At the conclusion of his *Letter to an Imaginary Friend,* McGrath offers a similar glimpse of the promised land: "The fields of a farm! / Must have been laid out like Grant Wood and Joan Miró."[52] Like Moses and Marx, these two comrades could not enter paradise, but they told us where it was from here.

Recognition

The purpose of The American Poetry Recovery Series is to bring to public attention poets who have suffered unjust neglect in American literature. Tom McGrath told me he held it against American poetry that Don Gordon's work had not found its due, particularly in that it could not be found in any of the major anthologies. The only exception, I should note, is Walter Lowenfels's *Poets of Today: A New American Anthology* (New York: International Publishers, 1964), which includes "The Kimono." McGrath was probably responsible for that, since Lowenfels acknowledges McGrath's assistance in collecting the work of West Coast poets. McGrath urged Gordon's poetry on younger writers, dedicated poems to him in many of his books, and mentioned him in *Letter to an Imaginary Friend:* "Don Gordon, who'd left his mountainy perch / To join us in the mysteries of the joyous season."[53] I was one of those younger writers, and with the publication of this collection I trust that McGrath's goal has finally been attained.

From the beginning, critical reception of Gordon's poetry has been sparse. Only two reviews appeared in major journals in the 1940s. While acknowledging that the poems in *Statement* deal with "an entire era in our historical experience," Mona Van Duyn wrote in *Poetry* that "Mr. Gordon is trying hard to make feeling and meaning out of his subject, to keep the imagination from being clipped short by the topical; but *Statement* is too accurate a description of its own contents. To make this statement an experience, the writer relies too heavily on the descriptive adjective. . . . Much more than that must be done with statement; it must not be decorated with imagery, it must arise out of it." Louis Townsend Nicholl dismissed Gordon in the *Saturday Review of Literature* with these words: "He has a few passages of magnificent language, as language . . . but in general he is a little pretentious, even bombastic, and not lucid."[54]

Gordon's third volume of poetry, published in the late 1950s, was not reviewed in any of the major journals, even though his work was occasionally printed in some of them, including *The American Scholar.* In addition to his blacklisting in Hollywood, which was personally disastrous, he was forced to suffer the more subtle exclusion from the literary world. After awhile, McGrath began referring to Don Gordon and Naomi Replansky as the "lost poets," a category that might have also included John Beecher, David Gallatin Cumberland, Olga Cabral, Frank Marshall Davis, and many others. It was only in the radical 1960s, through the efforts of Lowenfels and a few others, that the slow process of recovery began. Still, by 1978 the situation was not much improved, such that in his first letter to me Gordon wrote, "One never knows if one is read by *anybody*."[55]

The curious thing is that Gordon didn't feel lost but seemed largely content to have done the work for its own sake. He wrote to me concerning what he called the "forensic" aspects of literature, namely, "reading out loud in bookstores, selling books in person, trying to get into the public prints, soliciting reviews, generally hyping onself." His letter concludes: "To me everything outside the poem itself is just business. I don't object to anyone else doing all this to push their work. I just can't do it. I do work constantly to get it published, however."[56] Gordon was not an organizer; rather, he was a man of letters quite outside the college- and university-affiliated writing programs that began in the 1950s and proliferated in the 1960s. A shy man, "his interior sun proceeding / As usual on its path" ("The Silent"), he remained a close observer, absorbed in what was happening around him, assimilating the great social forces and symbols.

Once when he was traveling in Mexico, he was guided to his room in a small hotel by a maid who referred to him as *señor poeta* and said that it was an honor to have a poet stay there. Gordon was touched by the recognition. For him and many other poets—I count myself among them—these are rare and treasured moments.

In 1977, writing about *On the Ward* in *The Minnesota Review*, P. J. Laska confidently predicted that "literary imperialism is on the wane" and remarked that Gordon's "poems are strongest when they are close to home, and weakest when they wallow in weltschmerz." Laska continued: "There is no suggestion of a redemptive dialectic. . . . Here at the apex of alienation the symbol outweighs the man. . . . Only dead-end violence and surface realism have a place. A wilfull attitude beats back discovery."[57] Given the direction of American society in the decades since that review, it appears that Gordon was more accurate than Laska in predicting the national mentality and quality of life.

In the same issue of *The Minnesota Review*, a number of American writers responded to a questionnaire on the relationship between Marxism and the arts. Among them, in a rare "public appearance," Gordon responded:

> I do not believe that talking about a Marxist art will produce it. If it comes it can only come from the internal and external pressures of the individual plus whatever talent he has. Marxism can only inform the mind and provide an atmosphere in which an art of social value may grow. If there is anything that can be learned from the Thirties it is that art cannot be legislated into existence, it cannot be philosophized into existence. Any discussion or any critiques may be useful as stimuli but cannot be more. If a label like "Marxist" must be used, it should be used in the broadest possible sense, allowing for the value of any socially aware work or of any work that believes change is possible and progress conceivable. If there is any one criticism that can be aimed for art today, it is that it is unaware of the real world, makes no comment on it, and is mainly narrow and trivial.[58]

For his part, McGrath insisted that Marxism would have to be flexible and, above all, artistic to have any purpose or reality.[59]

In his last years, Gordon was happy to have his work included in *We Believe in Humanity* (1986), a large anthology of American democratic writers that was published only in Russian. Through the efforts of Georgi Zlobin, an eminent Soviet authority on American literature, this collection brought together work by McGrath, LeSueur, Truman Nelson, me, and many other writers neglected and suppressed in our own country. With an edition of fifty thousand copies, which at once sold out, this book provided probably the highest circulation many of us ever enjoyed for our work.

◇ ◇ ◇

Don Gordon was always close to the main currents of the twentieth century, most of which he lived through. His books reflect his concentration on world events, especially the epochal movements of revolution and counterrevolution. His recognition of the sheer strength of the latter (*pace* P. J. Laska) was distinctive. His early "masks" of leading communist and fascist dictators remain evocative of mighty forces being brought into continental conflict. Gordon lived through eras of mass murder, world wars, genocide, and the abiding threat of nuclear annihilation. It made no sense to him to divorce aesthetics from political existence: humankind had produced unprecedented economic and technological forces, but these threatened to escape beyond our control—or be used by an exploitative class to strengthen its authority.

In the late 1970s, when we midwestern radicals were much concerned to recover our militant cultural heritage, from the days of the Civil War through the heyday of the Socialist Party and the hunger marches of the 1930s, Gordon lodged a critical note: "Regionalism has a tendency to become narrow and often bucolic. [It] can form a firm base from which poets might take off. But regionalism seems to me, as such, to have had its day. The country and the world have long since passed it by as a basic source of stimuli for the writer."[60] I understood him to be encouraging an emphasis on world rather than local consciousness. With few exceptions, his poetry is not dependent on the place where he lived, though I believe that if we know his territory, we can better appreciate his poems. Gordon's work emerged from a vibrant West Coast radical culture that existed concomitantly in Los Angeles with the more celebrated glamour of Hollywood. Certainly, a creative genius like Rudolph Schindler was internationalist to the core of his being. And so was Don Gordon.

Through a fusion of Freud and Marx, at which he arrived independently, Gordon recognized and articulated how the external threat of war and annihilation was being replicated in the internal worlds of dreams and nightmares, out into the phantasmagoria of films and television, and beyond to the growing chaos of everyday life in America. He believed that conformity, repression, and alienation, so typical of 1950s America, would come back to haunt the nation. His later books reflected the collapse of civil society, marked, for instance, by the 1964 Watts riots and the uprising in South Central Los Angeles in 1992 following the acquittal of police officers in the notorious Rodney King case. Gordon saw the brutality of law and order, but he also recognized how the mass of people were oppressed by the conditions in which they lived. It is a pity that the emerging angry young poets of Los Angeles—such as Luis Rodriguez, their most eloquent spokesman—never connected with Don Gordon. Perhaps this volume of his collected work can be that bridge between generations. As he once observed, "All is not lost, just delayed."[61]

◇ ◇ ◇

It will take time to assess Don Gordon's true place in American poetry. With the exception of his family and a few close friends and fellow writers, he lived in isolation. The paradox is that he was nonetheless a close observer of the American scene, so eloquent about its cultural contradictions and social ills. He was influenced by Robinson Jeffers early on, and to a certain extent by the surrealists, but he felt that they were not adequate in offering ways out of real predicaments. In a time of decadence, he strove with great courage to preserve a healthy perspective.

Technically, Gordon's work is closest to that of radical modernist artists such as Max Ernst and Peter Blume as well as such "interior" poets as Tadeusz Rozewicz, who wrote:

that old woman who
is leading a goat by a rope
is more necessary
and more precious
than the seven wonders of the world
anyone who thinks and feels
that she is not necessary
is a mass murderer.[62]

In a comparison with South American poets, Gordon is more like the difficult, austere Cesar Vallejo than the public, declamatory Pablo Neruda. Gordon excelled in writing short poems, with his best rarely more than a page in length, as did his contemporary William Stafford, who shared Gordon's concern for ethics and the problems of their time. But unlike Stafford, who was appointed Poetry Consultant to the Library of Congress in 1970, Gordon neither sought nor received awards. Denying that she and Gordon were lost or neglected, LeSueur wrote to me: "No, we are the privileged, honored that we were not picked up by the whoremasters, into the big rings of bourgeois whorehouse culture. . . . Don Gordon is great because he speaks of all this so powerfully, reveals and exposes and shows the vigorous and wondrous strength of the people . . . [;] we have not been neglected, we have been secretly fed by the people more than we know. . . . We have also nourished each other . . . [;] we are the triumphant living. . . . We were faithful to our responsibility, unbuyable, uncorruptable and were nourished and got better under persecution . . . and are still here."[63] When he read LeSueur's letter and the first version of this essay, Gordon wrote: "I now see, for the first time, what I did through all these years. Yes, once in a while, I wondered if writing about movements and events was going to make it all dated. You have made me see that it is not—that it is a record of what one man saw and felt through these decades. And that it has a certain historical value, in a tiny way, hopefully for the young ones to come."[64] Now, at last, this volume provides an opportunity for readers especially in the United States to see Don Gordon's work as a whole, in all its disturbing depth, its remarkable range of themes, and its hope for our country.

NOTES

1. Thomas McGrath, "McGrath on McGrath," *North Dakota Quarterly* 50:4 (Fall 1982): 14.
2. Don Gordon, "Childhood," "Missing Person," and "An Old Radical," *Quindaro* 3 (Jan. 1979): 26–27.

3. "Panel on the Frontiers of Language," *Quindaro* 8–9 (1981): 27–34.

4. Don Gordon (hereafter DG) to Fred Whitehead (hereafter FW), Aug. 22, 1980.

5. DG to FW, Feb. 6, 1980.

6. Otherwise unattributed biographical information on DG (quoted or paraphrased) and certain information about his contemporaries were largely contributed by his stepdaughter, Tina Gainsboro, of Los Angeles during numerous conversations with me since 1986, from which I quote with her permission. Various supporting documents, such as DG's birth certificate, passport, and book contracts, are in her possession and were shared with me. Some details were provided by Don and Henrie Gordon during our conversations in 1986, which they gave me permission to quote or paraphrase in this essay. For additional information about the Gordons, see *Unamerican,* a short feature film released in 2002 by Tinderbox Pictures of Torrance, California, directed by Jesús D. Heredia.

7. Carey McWilliams, *Southern California Country* (New York: Duell, Sloan and Pearce, 1946), 270.

8. Stone is quoted in ibid., 275.

9. Official membership records of the League of American Writers were stolen in 1943, but its executive secretary, Franklin Folsom, includes DG in a reconstructed list of members in *Days of Anger, Days of Hope: A Memoir of the League of American Writers, 1937–1942* (Niwot: University Press of Colorado, 1994), 290. However, Folsom incorrectly gives DG's dates as 1911–74.

10. Nancy Lynn Schwartz, in *The Hollywood Writers' Wars* (New York: Knopf, 1982), focuses on the Screen Writers' Guild but provides a useful political and social context for the cultural Left in Los Angeles. *Highlights of a Fighting History: Sixty Years of the Communist Party USA* (New York: International Publishers, 1979) provides contemporary documents on the Communist Party. General histories include Harvey Klehr, *The Heyday of American Communism: The Depression Decade* (New York: Basic Books, 1984); and Fraser M. Ottanelli, *The Communist Party of the United States: From the Depression to World War II* (New Brunswick, N.J.: Rutgers University Press, 1991).

11. Eloquent, perceptive firsthand accounts of Schindler and Ain, respectively, are provided by Esther McCoy in *Five California Architects* (New York: Reinhold, 1960) and *The Second Generation* (Salt Lake City: Gibbs M. Smith, 1984).

12. Fenton is quoted in McWilliams, *Southern California Country,* 269.

13. *Writers' Congress: The Proceedings of the Conference held in October 1943 under the Sponsorship of the Hollywood Writers' Mobilization and the University of California* (Berkeley: University of California Press, 1944).

14. Berkeley's testimony was front-page news in the *Los Angeles Times,* Sept. 20, 1951. DG's photo was published in the same newspaper on Sept. 19. Berkeley's testimony naming DG is in *Hearings before the Committee on Un-American Activities: Communist Infiltration of Hollywood Motion Picture Industry,* pt. 4 (Washington, D.C.: U.S. Government Printing Office, 1951), 1582.

15. DG's testimony on Sept. 24 is in *Hearings,* pt. 5, 1785–93. Charlotte Darling Adams named DG in *Hearings,* pt. 6, 2310.

16. DG, *Hearings,* pt. 5.

17. The literature on the blacklist period is now voluminous. An excellent general survey is provided by DG's friend Cedric Belfrage in *The American Inquisition, 1945–1960* (New York: Thunder's Mouth, 1989). The best overall history for the film industry is Larry Ceplair and Steven Englund, *The Inquisition in Hollywood* (Berkeley: University of California Press, 1983; reprint, Urbana: University of Illinois Press, 2003). See also David Talbot and Barbara Zheutlin, *Creative Differences: Profiles of Hollywood Dissidents* (Boston: South End Press, 1978); Ann Fagan Ginger and David Christiano, eds., *The Cold War against Labor,* 2 vols. (Berkeley, Calif.: Meiklejohn Civil Liberties Institute, 1987); Bud Schultz and Ruth Schultz, *It Did Happen Here: Recollections of Political Repression in America* (Berkeley: University of California Press, 1989); Griffin Fariello, *Red Scare: Memories of the American Inquisition—An Oral History* (New York: W. W. Norton, 1995); and Patrick McGilligan and Paul Buhle, *Tender Comrades: A Backstory of the Hollywood Blacklist* (New York: St. Martin's Press, 1997). Prominent writers such as Ernest Hemingway, John Steinbeck, and W. H. Auden were targets of FBI surveillance, as documented by Herbert Mitgang in *Dangerous Dossiers: Exposing the Secret War against America's Authors* (New York: Donald I. Fine, 1988). The broad cultural crosscurrents affecting those involved in film production are illuminated in Paul Buhle and Dave Wagner, *Radical Hollywood* (New York: New Press, 2002).

18. McGrath's testimony is in *Hearings,* pt. 5, 859–64. His bitter description of the whole Los Angeles cultural environment is in pt. 2, sec. 2 of his *Letter to an Imaginary Friend* (Port Townsend, Wash.: Copper Canyon Press, 1997), 145–51.

19. Alice McGrath to FW, July 28, 1994.

20. Gene Frumkin, "A Note on Tom McGrath—The Early 50s," *North Dakota Quarterly* 50:4 (Fall 1982): 46–51.

21. Alvaro Cardona-Hine, "Knowing McGrath a Little," *North Dakota Quarterly* 50:4 (Fall 1982): 52–55.

22. Frumkin, "Note on Tom McGrath."

23. A good discussion of the cultural milieu of the *California Quarterly* is in Cary Nelson and Jefferson Hendricks, *Edwin Rolfe: A Biographical Essay and Guide to the Rolfe Archive at the University of Illinois at Urbana-Champaign* (Urbana: University of Illinois Library, 1990), 55–66. Rolfe, who died prematurely of a heart attack in 1954, was a close personal friend of the Gordons and of McGrath, who wrote a foreword to a posthumous volume of Rolfe's poetry, *Permit Me Refuge* (Los Angeles: California Quarterly, 1955). See also Edwin Rolfe, *Collected Poems,* ed. Cary Nelson and Jefferson Hendricks (Urbana: University of Illinois Press, 1993).

24. *California Quarterly* 1:1 (Fall 1951): inside cover.

25. McGrath, "McGrath on McGrath," 14.

26. Blurbs from the paperback edition of Thomas McGrath's *Letter to an Imaginary Friend, Parts 1 and 2* (Chicago: Swallow Press, 1970).

27. For more on Claude Williams, see Cedric Belfrage, *A Faith to Free the People* (New York: Dryden Press, 1944). This is an expanded version of *Let My People Go* (London: Left Book Club, 1939) and *South of God* (New York: Modern Age Books, 1941). The background of Williams and other southern religious activists is explored in Anthony P. Dunbar, *Against*

the American Grain: Southern Radicals and Prophets, 1929–1959 (Charlottesville: University Press of Virginia, 1981).

28. DG, "Hollywood Blacklist Oral History Transcript," Oral History Program, University of California at Los Angeles, 1988, interview by Larry Ceplair (hereafter cited as UCLA interview), pp. 31–32, 34–35, 36–37. Quoted by permission of the Regents of the University of California and the UCLA Oral History Program, Department of Special Collections, Charles E. Young Research Library.

29. Alice McGrath to FW, July 28, 1994.

30. UCLA interview, p. 59.

31. Ulrich Bischoff, *Max Ernst, 1891–1976: Beyond Painting* (Cologne: Benedikt Taschen, 1991), 43–44.

32. The theme of modernism in American radical poetry is discussed at length in Cary Nelson, *Repression and Recovery: Modern American Poetry and the Politics of Cultural Memory, 1910–1945* (Madison: University of Wisconsin Press, 1989). Curiously, Richard Candida Smith's ambitious *Utopia and Dissent: Art, Poetry, and Politics in California* (Berkeley: University of California Press, 1995), while concentrating on modernism in that state, entirely omits the *California Quarterly* group. Perhaps California is like Walt Whitman: large enough to contain multitudes, including divergent avant-garde groups that scarcely connect or interact. Stephen Schwartz's *From West to East: California and the Making of the American Mind* (New York: Free Press, 1998) is so violently anticommunist and concerned with scandal and intrigue that it is useless for understanding poetry like that by DG or his friends. The modernist context is profusely revealed in visual art contemporary with DG in Frances K. Pohl, *In the Eye of the Storm: An Art of Conscience, 1930–1970* (San Francisco: Pomegranate Artbooks, 1995).

33. Meridel LeSueur, "I Was Marching," *Ripening*, 2d ed. (New York: Feminist Press, 1990), 158–65.

34. Peter Weiss, *The Persecution and Assassination of Jean-Paul Marat* (New York: Pocket Books, 1966), 68.

35. UCLA interview, p. 59.

36. Bertolt Brecht, "To My Countrymen," *Poems, 1913–1956*, ed. John Willett and Ralph Manheim (New York: Methuen, 1976), 417.

37. Tadeusz Rozewicz, "It Was January," *"The Survivor" and Other Poems*, trans. Magnus J. Krynski and Robert A. Mcguire (Princeton, N.J.: Princeton University Press, 1976), 21.

38. For the connection between celebrity and psychoanalysis, see Stephen Farber and Marc Green, *Hollywood on the Couch* (New York: William Morrow, 1993).

39. John Beecher, "Screened," *Collected Poems, 1924–1974* (New York: Macmillan, 1974), 167–69.

40. David Riesman, *The Lonely Crowd* (New Haven, Conn.: Yale University Press, 1961), 16–25.

41. William Stafford, "At the Bomb Testing Site," *The Rescued Year* (New York: Harper and Row, 1966), 32; Hart Crane, "The River," *Complete Poems and Selected Letters and Prose*, ed. Brom Weber (New York: Liveright, 1966), 64.

42. Unidentified newspaper clipping, author's files.

43. William Blake, "To the Accuser Who Is the God of This World," *Complete Poetry and Prose,* ed. David V. Erdman (New York: Doubleday, 1965), 266.

44. Karl Marx, "The Eighteenth Brumaire of Louis Bonaparte," in vol. 1 of *Selected Works* (Moscow: Foreign Language Publishing House, 1958), 247.

45. Thomas McGrath, "Ode for the American Dead in Asia," *Selected Poems, 1938–1988* (Port Townsend, Wash.: Copper Canyon Press, 1988), 56–57.

46. Mike Davis, *City of Quartz: Excavating the Future in Los Angeles* (London: Verso, 1990), 224.

47. Robert Lowell, "For the Union Dead," *For the Union Dead* (New York: Farrar, Straus and Giroux, 1965), 72.

48. DG left instructions that his body should go to the UCLA Medical School, and his family respected his wishes. Thus, in 1977 the poet foresaw and described his own final destiny.

49. Charles Baudelaire, "Voyages," *Flowers of Evil* (New York: New Directions, 1955), 137.

50. Ibid.

51. Peter Blume (1906–92) is profiled in *Current Biography* (New York: H. H. WIlson, 1956), which reviews his complex artistic career to that date, including the clamor attending the exhibition of his large painting *The Eternal City* in 1937. His *Study for the Boulders of Avila* is reproduced in *ARTnews* (Mar. 1988): 195.

52. McGrath, *Letter to an Imaginary Friend* (1997 ed.), 398.

53. Ibid., 334.

54. Mona Van Duyn, review of *Statement* in *Poetry* 64 (June 1944): 171; Louis Townsend Nicholl, review of *Statement* in *Saturday Review of Literature* (Nov. 24, 1944): 24.

55. DG to FW, Sept. 15, 1978.

56. DG to FW, Dec. 30, 1983.

57. P. J. Laska, review of *On the Ward* in *The Minnesota Review* (n.s.) 9 (Fall 1977): 137.

58. Don Gordon's response in "A Fish Needs a Bicycle: Responses to a Questionnaire on Marxism and the Arts," *The Minnesota Review* (n.s.) 9 (Fall 1977): 19.

59. Thomas McGrath's response in ibid., 35–37.

60. DG to FW, Sept. 15, 1978.

61. DG to FW, May 30, 1982.

62. Rozewicz, "In the Midst of Life," *"The Survivor" and Other Poems,* 45.

63. Meridel LeSueur to FW, Dec. 28, 1983.

64. DG to FW, Feb. 15, 1984.

NOTES TO THE POEMS

STATEMENT

Epigraph to Part 1

The conservative poet T. S. Eliot used the rose as a traditional symbol of persisting Christian faith. The radical communist poet Hugh MacDiarmid counterposed the thistle, as the traditional symbol of Scotland, but also as an image of opposition to Anglo-Catholic conservatism.

"Sea"

This poem is based on DG's voyage from California to New York, via the Panama Canal, in 1927.

"The Wailing Wall"

Thought by some to be the only remnant of Solomon's Temple in Jerusalem, this massive wall is still visited by Orthodox Jews who lament its destruction by chanting prayers.

"Kronos"

Kronos is Greek for *time;* it is also the name of one of the Titans of early Greek mythology. As recounted in Hesiod's *Theogony,* Kronos was the son of Uranus, whom he castrated, throwing his genitals into the sea. Kronos, in turn, was slain by a thunderbolt hurled by his own son, Zeus. This myth survives today in the symbol of Father Time, with his scythe, seeing out the old year.

"Hunger March"

DG related that viewing such a march radicalized him during the Great Depression. The 1930s saw a number of local, state, and national hunger marches, beginning with one on March 6, 1930, that was organized by the Communist Party and its allies.

"Sargasso"

The Sargasso Sea, a calm section of the North Atlantic Ocean west of the Azores, is characterized by floating seaweed (*sargassum*). Hence, *sargasso* refers to any zone of oozy, turbid melancholy.

"Underground, 1935"

Between February 11 and 15, 1934, the Austrian government and paramilitary Heimwehr forces bombarded the Karl Marx Hof in Vienna, a housing development and socialist stronghold. This effectively broke the Left, preparing the way for a Nazi coup attempt on

July 25 in which the Christian Socialist Engelbert Dollfuss was assassinated and leading eventually to the annexation of Austria by Nazi Germany in March 1938.

"Testament"

"We are breaking the superstructure": The German philosopher Karl Marx posited the idea that in society a political and cultural superstructure is erected on a base of social and economic relations.

"We Speak of Action"

"Denmark . . . Elsinore": William Shakespeare's *Hamlet* is set in Elsinore Castle in Denmark.

"With his headsman": In Japan and Germany, fascists revived the medieval form of execution by beheading. *The Axe of Wandsbek* (1947) by Arnold Zweig is a fictional treatment of such an executioner.

"Love Song, 1938"

Alfried Krupp, a prominent German steel manufacturer, was brought to trial by the U.S. Army after World War II and convicted of war crimes, including the use of slave labor. Skoda, Vickers, Schneider-Creusot, and Du Pont (erroneously rendered by DG as "duPont") were wartime arms manufacturers in Europe and the United States.

"The Departure"

Epigraph: This is a quotation from the *Communist Manifesto.*

"Dialectic"

The modern concept of the dialectic was developed by the German philosopher G. W. F. Hegel as a process by which transformational change moved through three historic stages: thesis, antithesis, and synthesis. While Hegel's theory was idealist, Marx proposed "turning it on its head," arguing that fundamental revolutions have a materialist social and economic basis ("From the Afterword to the Second German Edition of the First Volume of *Capital,*" in vol. 1 of *Selected Works* [Moscow: Foreign Languages Publishing House, 1958], 456).

"Lenin"

"The moaning colonies": Contrasted with the more moderate socialists, the communists under Lenin placed a strong emphasis on the liberation of colonies from imperial rule. This led militants such as Ho Chi Minh to join the communist movement.

"Hitler"

"dead Wotan": The Nazis developed medievalist and archaic rituals celebrating ancient pagan gods, including Wotan, the subject of a disturbing essay by the Swiss psychologist Carl Jung in 1936 (see *The Collected Works of C. G. Jung,* ed. and trans. Gerhard Adler and R. F. C. Hull, vol. 10 [Princeton, N.J.: Princeton University Press, 1970]).

"Mussolini"

"The taurine head": That is, like a bull's head. The painting *The Eternal City* by Peter Blume was first exhibited in New York City in 1937 and includes a brutish glaring head of Mussolini. Pablo Picasso's painting *Guernica* similarly incorporates the head of a bull as a symbol of fascist rage and destructive power.

"The bound ax": The *fasces* of imperial Rome—an ax surrounded by rods—became the official symbol of fascist Italy, representing the punitive authority of the state.

"African graves": Mussolini invaded Libya in 1930 and Ethiopia in 1935.

"Matteotti": Giacomo Matteotti, a socialist deputy in the Italian parliament, was murdered by fascists on June 10, 1924. Two years later the perpetrators were either acquitted or given light sentences.

"The Headsman in Evening Clothes"

On the headsman image, see the note to "We Speak of Action" (above).

"death is in their image": The Schutzstaffel (SS) in Germany adopted the Death's Head as its symbol, and one unit of this elite guard was known as the Death's Head Division.

"The Poet in the Stone House"

Robinson Jeffers built Tor House, his residence in Carmel, California, from stones brought in from the nearby shore. DG acknowledged Jeffers as the most important influence on his own poetry, though here he argues against the elder poet's chthonic misanthropy.

CIVILIAN POEMS

"The Sealed Train"

In April 1917, Lenin and other Bolsheviks were transported in a sealed railroad car from Zurich through Germany to Stockholm by the German government, which hoped that Lenin would disrupt the fledgling government of Aleksandr Fyodorovich Kerensky in Russia. The title of Edmund Wilson's book *To the Finland Station* (1940) refers to Lenin's dramatic arrival in St. Petersburg.

"the dark people": This was a traditional phrase for the lower classes of workers and peasants.

"Communiqué"

Lewisite is a type of poison gas named after the American chemist Winford Lee Lewis.

"Laocoön"

Laocoön was a Trojan who insulted Apollo and was strangled to death, along with his two sons, by sea serpents. This mythological event was depicted in a classical statue that was excavated in Rome in 1506.

"The Conqueror"

"their Baedeker": Baedeker was a publisher of nineteenth-century travel guides for various European cities.

"The Antennae"

"the tar pits": This is a reference to the La Brea tar pits in downtown Los Angeles, in which the remains of numerous predators such as saber-toothed tigers were found.

"The Warhead"

"V-1 / V-2": These were powerful long-range German rockets that destroyed sections of London during World War II.

DISPLACED PERSONS

"The Hunted"

"The one who walks in the river": A fragment from Heraclitus, the Greek philosopher who exalted the concept of change sweeping through the entire universe. See "Heracleitus: On the Universe" in volume 4 of Hippocrates' *Works*, trans. W. H. S. Jones (Cambridge, Mass.: Harvard University Press, 1931), 483.

"He considered the meek": This is a reference to Jesus Christ.

"or said the earth was round": The Alexandrian scholar Eratosthenes demonstrated that the earth was curved.

"he taught the young men in the cypress grove": This is a reference to the Greek philosopher Socrates.

"or listed / the ape's ascending bone": This is a reference to the English naturalist Charles Darwin.

"he entered the dream": This is a reference to the Austrian psychoanalyst Sigmund Freud.

"found laws in the lungs of the English weavers": This is a reference to Marx, who published his intensive studies of government records of industrial conditions and the laws of capitalist political economy in *Das Capital* (1867).

"The Neurotics"

"we rode / On a rocking horse in the attic": This is an allusion to the D. H. Lawrence story "The Rocking-Horse Winner" (1926).

"Death of the Architect"

"R.M.S.": Rudolf M. Schindler was a founder of modern architecture in Los Angeles who redesigned DG's house after it was damaged by freeway construction. Schindler's work was notable for "experiments with flowing interior spaces, sleeping porches, the use of concrete and glass" (*Who's Who in Architecture from 1400 to the Present,* ed. J. M. Richards [New York: Holt, Rinehart and Winston, 1977], s.v. "Schindler, Rudolf M.").

"The Middle Passage"

"the physician": This is a reference to Victor Nasatir, one of DG's close friends who died of a massive heart attack.

"the architect": This is a reference to Schindler. See the note for "Death of the Architect" (above).

"the poet": This is a reference to Edwin Rolfe, a veteran of the Spanish Civil War and the author of several volumes of poetry.

"When the Time Comes"

"ormolu": Ormolu is metalwork of copper and tin alloys that resembles gold. It thus suggests decoration that is elaborate and ornate, but artificial.

ON THE WARD

"Defoliation"

During the Vietnam War, U.S. military aircraft sprayed poisonous chemicals over the country's jungles in order to deprive the Communists of ground cover. Among these chemicals was Agent Orange, which proved highly toxic to humans as well as plants and harmed not only the enemy and innocent Vietnamese civilians but also U.S. military personnel.

"Kamikaze"

In the late phases of World War II in the Pacific, including at Pearl Harbor, Japanese pilots undertook suicide attacks, flying their airplanes fully loaded with bombs into U.S. ships.

"The young monks in saffron robes / Burned in the cruel light": During the Vietnam War, Buddhist monks committed suicide by immolation to protest the destruction of their country.

"The Reichstag Fires"

On February 27, 1933, the Nazis set fire to the Reichstag in Berlin, the center of parliamentary government, but charged the Communists with the crime. Subsequently, brutal repression began against German Social Democrats, Jews, and Gypsies, as well as Communist Party members.

"Tableau Vivant"

A *tableau vivant* (French for "living picture") is a stage scene in which costumed actors remain silent and motionless.

"Castor and Pollux": These twins were born to Leda, who was impregnated by Zeus in the form of a swan, and became a constellation of paired stars.

"Samizdat"

Samizdat is the underground literature of the former Soviet Union, especially between 1950 and 1990. Various dissenting authors either concealed their writings or sometimes had them published abroad.

"Altamira": This cave in northwest Spain is notable for its large prehistoric wall paintings.

"Yenan": This was the headquarters for the Red Army in northwest China in the late 1930s.

"Wounded Knee": This was the South Dakota site of a massacre of Lakota by the U.S. Army in the winter of 1890. An armed Indian uprising also occurred there in 1973.

"The Underground Railroad"

The Underground Railroad was a secret interracial network that operated throughout the United States before the Civil War to convey slaves to freedom in the North and Canada.

"one Dred Scott": Dred Scott was a slave who argued in federal court that when he was taken to a free state by his master he was thereby freed. Chief Justice Roger Taney of the U.S. Supreme Court wrote the 1857 opinion against Scott, declaring that slaves "had no rights which the white man was bound to respect," provoking widespread popular indignation in the North.

"Memorial Day"

"the whole thing / Blew down the Yalu that December": In December 1950, Chinese Communist troops poured south past the Yalu River into North Korea, forcing a dramatic retreat of U.S.-led forces.

"We Are Not Ready"

"A fantasy in glazed ware, / Around and around an urn": This is an allusion to John Keats's poem "Ode on a Grecian Urn" (1820).

EXCAVATIONS

"The Archaeologist"

"He needs a Rosetta stone": This large tablet dating from 196 B.C. was discovered in Egypt in 1799. It features parallel texts of Egyptian hieroglyphics and Greek. A comparison of the texts by the scholar François Champollion led to a system for deciphering these and other Egyptian hieroglyphics whose meaning was previously unknown in modern times.

"Plateaus"

"the sky city of Acoma": An ancient city in western New Mexico, Acoma was called the "sky city" because it was built on a high outcrop of rock that afforded a dramatic vista of the surrounding countryside. It is one of the oldest continually inhabited communities in North America. DG and his wife visited this and other sites during a vacation in that part of the United States.

"The Shtetl"

During the czarist era, Jews in Russia were forced to live in isolated, segregated villages. They were often dependent on crafts or trades such as shoe or textile manufacturing for their livelihoods and were subject to raids by Cossacks and other paramilitary units.

"Graffiti"

"El grito de los angeles perdidos": This is Spanish for "the cry of the lost angels."

"The Mugging"

"Spengler's autumnal cities": Oswald Spengler was the author of *The Decline of the West* (1918–22), a gloomy but influential analysis of power and decadence in Western civilization.

"Kristallnacht"

On the night of November 9, 1938, two days after the assassination in Paris of a Nazi official by a young Jewish radical, Nazi gangs assaulted Jews, burned shops and synagogues, and otherwise intensified a reign of terror that was to last until their total defeat in 1945. *Kristallnacht* is German for "crystal night."

"2000"

DG wrote this poem for his great-granddaughter Taylor Hope Burke, who responded with the poem "1999," published in May 1999 in *Attic Salt,* the student literary journal of Loyola Marymount University.

THE SEA OF TRANQUILITY

"In the Vanguard"

"Lashed the gold changers": This is a reference to Jesus Christ.

"Insisted the earth moved around the sun": This is a reference to the Polish astronomer Nicolaus Copernicus.

"Announced the ascent of animals": This is a reference to Darwin.

"Opened the collective": This is a reference to Marx.

"Masada": The final stronghold of Jewish militants who in A.D. 73 committed suicide rather than surrender to the Roman army, Masada has been excavated by archaeologists.

"Waiting"

"waiting for lefty": This is a reference to the play *Waiting for Lefty* (1935) by Clifford Odets.

"or godot": This is a reference to the play *Waiting for Godot* (1952) by Samuel Beckett.

"Los Desaparecidos"

"Dónde están los desaparecidos?" This is Spanish for "Where are the disappeared?" In Guatemala, El Salvador, Chile, Brazil, Colombia, and Argentina between 1954 and the present, women have campaigned to learn the fate of their children who were seized and often murdered by the police, the army, or right-wing paramilitary groups.

A DON GORDON BIBLIOGRAPHY

BOOKS OF POEMS

Statement. Boston: Bruce Humphreys, 1943.

"Acknowledgment is made to *Frontier & Midland; Menorah Journal; New Caravan; New Masses; New Republic; N.Y. Herald-Tribune Books; Poetry, A Magazine of Verse; Prairie Schooner; Southern Review,* and other publications in which certain of these poems were first printed."

Reviewed by Lewis Townsend Nichol in *Saturday Review of Literature* 27 (November 24, 1944): 24; and Mona Van Duyn in *Poetry* 64 (June 1944): 171.

Civilian Poems. New York: The Beechhurst Press/Bernard Ackerman, 1946. (Combined with Aaaron Kramer, *The Glass Mountain and Other Poems.*)

"Acknowledgment is made to *The American Scholar; Asia; Experiment; Free World; Harper's Magazine; New Masses; The New Mexico Quarterly Review; The New Republic; Poetry* (Chicago); *Quarterly Review of Literature; The Saturday Review of Literature* and other publications in which certain of these poems were first printed."

Displaced Persons. Denver: Alan Swallow, 1958.

"Acknowledgment is made to the following publications in which many of these poems were first printed: *Accent; The American Scholar; The Antioch Review; California Quarterly; Coastlines; Contemporary Reader; Harper's Magazine; The Nation; Poetry* (Chicago); *The Saturday Review; Southwest Review; The Western Review.*"

On The Ward. Reno: West Coast Poetry Review, 1977.

"Acknowledgment is made to the following magazines in which some of these poems were first published: *Dacotah Territory; Green River Review; Grove; Harper's Magazine; Icarus; The Nation; North Country Anvil; The North Stone Review; Northern Light; Poetry; Poetry View; Praxis; Southern Voices; The Texas Quarterly; West Coast Poetry Review; West End; Xanadu.*"

Reviewed by P. J. Laska in *The Minnesota Review* (n.s.) 9 (Fall 1977): 136–37; and Fred Whitehead in *Quindaro* 3 (January 1979): 42.

Excavations. Reno: West Coast Poetry Review, 1979.

"Acknowledgment is made to the following magazines in which some of these poems were first published: *Blue Unicorn; Colorado Quarterly; Dacotah Territory; The Gramercy Review; The Greenfield Review; Harper's Magazine; Harvest Quarterly; Icarus; New Earth Review; New Kent Quarterly; The New Quarterly; Neworld; North Country Anvil; Poetry*

View; Praxis; Quindaro; Rocky Mountain Review; San Marcos Review; Snowy Egret; Stone Country; Texas Quarterly."

Reviewed by Fred Whitehead in *Daily World,* September 30, 1980.

The Sea of Tranquility. Willimantic, Conn.: Curbstone Press, 1989.
"Acknowledgment is made to the following magazines in which some of these poems were first printed: *Blue Unicorn, The Centennial Review, Electrum, The Gramercy Review, International Poetry Review, The Minnesota Review, North Dakota Quarterly, Puetro Del Sol, Quindaro, Samisdat, The San Fernando Poetry Journal.*"

Reviewed by Pat Hickerson in *People's Daily World,* June 23, 1989; and Dale Jacobson in *North Dakota Quarterly* 58.2 (Spring 1990): 167–69.

POEMS REPRINTED IN ANTHOLOGIES

"The Kimono": *Poets of Today: A New American Anthology.* Ed. Walter Lowenfels. New York: International Publishers, 1964. 59–60.

"The Archaeologist," "Ancestors," "The Ox," "Flight," "Bicentennial," "The Seventh Sense," "Childhood," "2000," "Rootless," "Free Fall," and "Ruins": *We Believe in Humanity* (in Russian). Eds. Georgi Zlobin and Oxana Kirichenko. Moscow: Raduga, 1986. 511–18.

"The Dissenter," "The Travelers," "The Investigation," "At the Station," "Consider the Meaning of Love," and "The Middle Passage": *Poets of the Non-Existent City: Los Angeles Poets in the McCarthy Years and After.* Ed. Estelle Gershogoren Novak. Albuquerque: University of New Mexico Press, 2002. 92–99.

TITLE INDEX

Don Gordon graduated Phi Beta Kappa from Pomona College in 1923, briefly attended law school, and then started reading scripts for Hollywood while helping studio workers organize into a union. Although he was blacklisted during the McCarthy era, his poems were published in such distinguished journals as *The American Scholar, Harpers, The Nation, Poetry, Prairie Schooner,* and *New Masses.* He died in Los Angeles in 1989.

Fred Whitehead is the author or editor of a number of scholarly articles and books on intellectual and cultural history, including *Freethought on the American Frontier* (1992).

The American Poetry Recovery Series

Collected Poems *Edwin Rolfe; edited by Cary Nelson and Jefferson Hendricks*
Trees Became Torches: Selected Poems *Edwin Rolfe; edited by Cary Nelson and Jefferson Hendricks*
Palace-Burner: The Selected Poetry of Sarah Piatt *Edited and with an Introduction by Paula Bernat Bennett*
Black Moods: Collected Poems *Frank Marshall Davis; edited by John Edgar Tidwell*
Rendezvous with Death: American Poems of the Great War *Edited by Mark W. Van Wienen*
The Wound and the Dream: Sixty Years of American Poems about the Spanish Civil War *Edited by Cary Nelson*
Collected Poems *Don Gordon; edited and with an Essay by Fred Whitehead*

The University of Illinois Press
is a founding member of the
Association of American University Presses.

Composed in 9/14 Meta
with Meta display
by Jim Proefrock
at the University of Illinois Press
Designed by Paula Newcomb
Manufactured by Sheridan Books, Inc.

University of Illinois Press
1325 South Oak Street
Champaign, IL 61820-6903
www.press.uillinois.edu